THE OEDIPUS CYCLE

DUDLEY FITTS and ROBERT FITZGERALD,
in addition to their translations of Sophocles,
collaborated on a new English version
of *The Alcestis of Euripides* (1936).
English versions of Aristophanes by Dudley Fitts are:
Lysistrata (1954), *The Frogs* (1955), *The Birds* (1957), and
Ladies' Day (1959).

SOPHOCLES

The Oedipus Cycle

AN ENGLISH VERSION

OEDIPUS REX
Dudley Fitts and Robert Fitzgerald

OEDIPUS AT COLONUS
Robert Fitzgerald

ANTIGONE
Dudley Fitts and Robert Fitzgerald

A Harvest/HBJ Book
Harcourt Brace Jovanovich, Publishers
San Diego   New York   London

RR SS TT UU

ISBN 0-15-683838-9

PRINTED IN THE UNITED STATES OF AMERICA

CONTENTS

ᛋ Oedipus Rex

AN ENGLISH VERSION
BY DUDLEY FITTS AND ROBERT FITZGERALD

FOR CLARA SEYMOUR ST. JOHN

πῶς δ' οὐκ ἀρίστη; τίς δ' εναντιώσεται;
τί χρὴ γενέσθαι τὴν ὑπερβεβλημένην
γυναῖκα;

PERSONS REPRESENTED*

OEDIPUS
A PRIEST
CREON
TEIRESIAS
IOCASTE
MESSENGER
SHEPHERD OF LAÏOS
SECOND MESSENGER
CHORUS OF THEBAN ELDERS

THE SCENE. *Before the palace of Oedipus, King of Thebes. A central door and two lateral doors open onto a platform which runs the length of the façade. On the platform, right and left, are altars; and three steps lead down into the "orchestra," or chorus-ground. At the beginning of the action these steps are crowded by suppliants who have brought branches and chaplets of olive leaves and who lie in various attitudes of despair.* OEDIPUS *enters.*

⋅§ PROLOGUE

OEDIPUS:

My children, generations of the living
In the line of Kadmos, nursed at his ancient hearth:
Why have you strewn yourselves before these altars
In supplication, with your boughs and garlands?
The breath of incense rises from the city
With a sound of prayer and lamentation.

Children,
I would not have you speak through messengers,
And therefore I have come myself to hear you—
I, Oedipus, who bear the famous name.

[*To a* PRIEST:
You, there, since you are eldest in the company,
Speak for them all, tell me what preys upon you,
Whether you come in dread, or crave some blessing:
Tell me, and never doubt that I will help you
In every way I can; I should be heartless
Were I not moved to find you suppliant here.

PRIEST:

Great Oedipus, O powerful King of Thebes!
You see how all the ages of our people
Cling to your altar steps: here are boys
Who can barely stand alone, and here are priests
By weight of age, as I am a priest of God,
And young men chosen from those yet unmarried;
As for the others, all that multitude,
They wait with olive chaplets in the squares,
At the two shrines of Pallas, and where Apollo
Speaks in the glowing embers.

Your own eyes
Must tell you: Thebes is tossed on a murdering sea
And can not lift her head from the death surge.
A rust consumes the buds and fruits of the earth;
The herds are sick; children die unborn,
And labor is vain. The god of plague and pyre
Raids like detestable lightning through the city,
And all the house of Kadmos is laid waste,
All emptied, and all darkened: Death alone
Battens upon the misery of Thebes.

You are not one of the immortal gods, we know;
Yet we have come to you to make our prayer
As to the man surest in mortal ways

And wisest in the ways of God. You saved us
From the Sphinx, that flinty singer, and the tribute
We paid to her so long; yet you were never
Better informed than we, nor could we teach you:
It was some god breathed in you to set us free.

Therefore, O mighty King, we turn to you:
Find us our safety, find us a remedy,
Whether by counsel of the gods or men.
A king of wisdom tested in the past
Can act in a time of troubles, and act well.
Noblest of men, restore
Life to your city! Think how all men call you
Liberator for your triumph long ago;
Ah, when your years of kingship are remembered,
Let them not say *We rose, but later fell*—
Keep the State from going down in the storm!
Once, years ago, with happy augury,
You brought us fortune; be the same again!
No man questions your power to rule the land:
But rule over men, not over a dead city!
Ships are only hulls, citadels are nothing,
When no life moves in the empty passageways.

OEDIPUS:

Poor children! You may be sure I know
All that you longed for in your coming here.
I know that you are deathly sick; and yet,
Sick as you are, not one is as sick as I.
Each of you suffers in himself alone
His anguish, not another's; but my spirit
Groans for the city, for myself, for you.

I was not sleeping, you are not waking me.
No, I have been in tears for a long while
And in my restless thought walked many ways.
In all my search, I found one helpful course,

And that I have taken: I have sent Creon,
Son of Menoikeus, brother of the Queen,
To Delphi, Apollo's place of revelation,
To learn there, if he can,
What act or pledge of mine may save the city.
I have counted the days, and now, this very day,
I am troubled, for he has overstayed his time.
What is he doing? He has been gone too long.
Yet whenever he comes back, I should do ill
To scant whatever duty God reveals.

PRIEST:

It is a timely promise. At this instant
They tell me Creon is here.

OEDIPUS:

O Lord Apollo!
May his news be fair as his face is radiant!

PRIEST:

It could not be otherwise: he is crowned with bay,
The chaplet is thick with berries.

OEDIPUS:

We shall soon know;
He is near enough to hear us now.

[*Enter* CREON
O Prince:
Brother: son of Menoikeus:
What answer do you bring us from the god?

CREON:

A strong one. I can tell you, great afflictions
Will turn out well, if they are taken well.

OEDIPUS:

What was the oracle? These vague words
Leave me still hanging between hope and fear.

CREON:

Is it your pleasure to hear me with all these
Gathered around us? I am prepared to speak,
But should we not go in?

OEDIPUS:

Let them all hear it.
It is for them I suffer, more than for myself.

CREON:

Then I will tell you what I heard at Delphi.

In plain words
The god commands us to expel from the land of
Thebes
An old defilement we are sheltering.
It is a deathly thing, beyond cure;
We must not let it feed upon us longer.

OEDIPUS:

What defilement? How shall we rid ourselves of it?

CREON:

By exile or death, blood for blood. It was
Murder that brought the plague-wind on the city.

OEDIPUS:

Murder of whom? Surely the god has named him?

CREON:

My lord: long ago Laïos was our king,
Before you came to govern us.

OEDIPUS:

I know;
I learned of him from others; I never saw him.

CREON:

> He was murdered; and Apollo commands us now
> To take revenge upon whoever killed him.

OEDIPUS:

> Upon whom? Where are they? Where shall we find a
>   clue
> To solve that crime, after so many years?

CREON:

> Here in this land, he said.
>   If we make enquiry,
> We may touch things that otherwise escape us.

OEDIPUS:

> Tell me: Was Laïos murdered in his house,
> Or in the fields, or in some foreign country?

CREON:

> He said he planned to make a pilgrimage.
> He did not come home again.

OEDIPUS:

>   And was there no one,
> No witness, no companion, to tell what happened?

CREON:

> They were all killed but one, and he got away
> So frightened that he could remember one thing only.

OEDIPUS:

> What was that one thing? One may be the key
> To everything, if we resolve to use it.

CREON:

> He said that a band of highwaymen attacked them,
> Outnumbered them, and overwhelmed the King.

OEDIPUS:

Strange, that a highwayman should be so daring—
Unless some faction here bribed him to do it.

CREON:

We thought of that. But after Laïos' death
New troubles arose and we had no avenger.

OEDIPUS:

What troubles could prevent your hunting down the
    killers?

CREON:

The riddling Sphinx's song
Made us deaf to all mysteries but her own.

OEDIPUS:

Then once more I must bring what is dark to light.
It is most fitting that Apollo shows,
As you do, this compunction for the dead.
You shall see how I stand by you, as I should,
To avenge the city and the city's god,
And not as though it were for some distant friend,
But for my own sake, to be rid of evil.
Whoever killed King Laïos might—who knows?—
Decide at any moment to kill me as well.
By avenging the murdered king I protect myself.

Come, then, my children: leave the altar steps,
Lift up your olive boughs!
                                    One of you go
And summon the people of Kadmos to gather here.
I will do all that I can; you may tell them that.
                                    [*Exit a* PAGE

So, with the help of God,
We shall be saved—or else indeed we are lost.

PRIEST:

Let us rise, children. It was for this we came,
And now the King has promised it himself.
Phoibos has sent us an oracle; may he descend
Himself to save us and drive out the plague.

> [*Exeunt* OEDIPUS *and* CREON *into the palace by the central door. The* PRIEST *and the* SUPPLIANTS *disperse R and L. After a short pause the* CHORUS *enters the orchestra.*

✤§ PÁRODOS

CHORUS:

[STROPHE 1

What is God singing in his profound
Delphi of gold and shadow?
What oracle for Thebes, the sunwhipped city?

Fear unjoints me, the roots of my heart tremble.

Now I remember, O Healer, your power, and wonder:
Will you send doom like a sudden cloud, or weave it
Like nightfall of the past?

Speak, speak to us, issue of holy sound:
Dearest to our expectancy: be tender!

[ANTISTROPHE 1

Let me pray to Athenê, the immortal daughter of
    Zeus,
And to Artemis her sister
Who keeps her famous throne in the market ring,

And to Apollo, bowman at the far butts of heaven—

O gods, descend! Like three streams leap against
The fires of our grief, the fires of darkness;
Be swift to bring us rest!

As in the old time from the brilliant house
Of air you stepped to save us, come again!

Now our afflictions have no end,   [STROPHE 2
Now all our stricken host lies down
And no man fights off death with his mind;

The noble plowland bears no grain,
And groaning mothers can not bear—

See, how our lives like birds take wing,
Like sparks that fly when a fire soars,
To the shore of the god of evening.

The plague burns on, it is pitiless,   [ANTISTROPHE 2
Though pallid children laden with death
Lie unwept in the stony ways,

And old gray women by every path
Flock to the strand about the altars

There to strike their breasts and cry
Worship of Phoibos in wailing prayers:
Be kind, God's golden child!

                                 [STROPHE 3
There are no swords in this attack by fire,
No shields, but we are ringed with cries.

Send the besieger plunging from our homes
Into the vast sea-room of the Atlantic
Or into the waves that foam eastward of Thrace—

For the day ravages what the night spares—

Destroy our enemy, lord of the thunder!
Let him be riven by lightning from heaven!

[ANTISTROPHE 3

Phoîbos Apollo, stretch the sun's bowstring,
That golden cord, until it sing for us,
Flashing arrows in heaven!

Artemis, Huntress,
Race with flaring lights upon our mountains!

O scarlet god, O golden-banded brow,
O Theban Bacchos in a storm of Maenads,

[Enter OEDIPUS, C.

Whirl upon Death, that all the Undying hate!
Come with blinding torches, come in joy!

◆§ SCENE I

OEDIPUS:

Is this your prayer? It may be answered. Come,
Listen to me, act as the crisis demands,
And you shall have relief from all these evils.

Until now I was a stranger to this tale,
As I had been a stranger to the crime.
Could I track down the murderer without a clue?
But now, friends,
As one who became a citizen after the murder,
I make this proclamation to all Thebans:

If any man knows by whose hand Laïos, son of Lab-
    dakos,
Met his death, I direct that man to tell me everything,
No matter what he fears for having so long withheld
    it.
Let it stand as promised that no further trouble
Will come to him, but he may leave the land in
    safety.

Moreover: If anyone knows the murderer to be for-
    eign,
Let him not keep silent: he shall have his reward from
    me.
However, if he does conceal it; if any man
Fearing for his friend or for himself disobeys this
    edict,
Hear what I propose to do:

I solemnly forbid the people of this country,
Where power and throne are mine, ever to receive
    that man
Or speak to him, no matter who he is, or let him
Join in sacrifice, lustration, or in prayer.
I decree that he be driven from every house,
Being, as he is, corruption itself to us: the Delphic
Voice of Zeus has pronounced this revelation.
Thus I associate myself with the oracle
And take the side of the murdered king.

As for the criminal, I pray to God—
Whether it be a lurking thief, or one of a number—
I pray that that man's life be consumed in evil and
    wretchedness.
And as for me, this curse applies no less
If it should turn out that the culprit is my guest here,
Sharing my hearth.
                You have heard the penalty.

I lay it on you now to attend to this
For my sake, for Apollo's, for the sick
Sterile city that heaven has abandoned.
Suppose the oracle had given you no command:
Should this defilement go uncleansed for ever?
You should have found the murderer: your king,
A noble king, had been destroyed!
                                        Now I,
Having the power that he held before me,
Having his bed, begetting children there
Upon his wife, as he would have, had he lived—
Their son would have been my children's brother,
If Laïos had had luck in fatherhood!
(But surely ill luck rushed upon his reign)—
I say I take the son's part, just as though
I were his son, to press the fight for him
And see it won! I'll find the hand that brought
Death to Labdakos' and Polydoros' child,
Heir of Kadmos' and Agenor's line.
And as for those who fail me,
May the gods deny them the fruit of the earth,
Fruit of the womb, and may they rot utterly!
Let them be wretched as we are wretched, and worse!

For you, for loyal Thebans, and for all
Who find my actions right, I pray the favor
Of justice, and of all the immortal gods.

CHORAGOS:

Since I am under oath, my lord, I swear
I did not do the murder, I can not name
The murderer. Might not the oracle
That has ordained the search tell where to find him?

OEDIPUS:

An honest question. But no man in the world
Can make the gods do more than the gods will.

CHORAGOS:

There is one last expedient—

OEDIPUS:

Tell me what it is.
Though it seem slight, you must not hold it back.

CHORAGOS:

A lord clairvoyant to the lord Apollo,
As we all know, is the skilled Teiresias.
One might learn much about this from him, Oedipus.

OEDIPUS:

I am not wasting time:
Creon spoke of this, and I have sent for him—
Twice, in fact; it is strange that he is not here.

CHORAGOS:

The other matter—that old report—seems useless.

OEDIPUS:

Tell me. I am interested in all reports.

CHORAGOS:

The King was said to have been killed by highway-
men.

OEDIPUS:

I know. But we have no witnesses to that.

CHORAGOS:

If the killer can feel a particle of dread,
Your curse will bring him out of hiding!

OEDIPUS:

No.
The man who dared that act will fear no curse.
[*Enter the blind seer* TEIRESIAS, *led by a* PAGE

CHORAGOS:

> But there is one man who may detect the criminal.
> This is Teiresias, this is the holy prophet
> In whom, alone of all men, truth was born.

OEDIPUS:

> Teiresias: seer: student of mysteries,
> Of all that's taught and all that no man tells,
> Secrets of Heaven and secrets of the earth:
> Blind though you are, you know the city lies
> Sick with plague; and from this plague, my lord,
> We find that you alone can guard or save us.
>
> Possibly you did not hear the messengers?
> Apollo, when we sent to him,
> Sent us back word that this great pestilence
> Would lift, but only if we established clearly
> The identity of those who murdered Laïos.
> They must be killed or exiled.
>   Can you use
> Birdflight or any art of divination
> To purify yourself, and Thebes, and me
> From this contagion? We are in your hands.
> There is no fairer duty
> Than that of helping others in distress.

TEIRESIAS:

> How dreadful knowledge of the truth can be
> When there's no help in truth! I knew this well,
> But made myself forget. I should not have come.

OEDIPUS:

> What is troubling you? Why are your eyes so cold?

TEIRESIAS:

> Let me go home. Bear your own fate, and I'll
> Bear mine. It is better so: trust what I say.

OEDIPUS:

What you say is ungracious and unhelpful
To your native country. Do not refuse to speak.

TEIRESIAS:

When it comes to speech, your own is neither tem-
    perate
Nor opportune. I wish to be more prudent.

OEDIPUS:

In God's name, we all beg you—

TEIRESIAS:

                                            You are all ignorant.
No; I will never tell you what I know.
Now it is my misery; then, it would be yours.

OEDIPUS:

What! You do know something, and will not tell us?
You would betray us all and wreck the State?

TEIRESIAS:

I do not intend to torture myself, or you
Why persist in asking? You will not persuade me.

OEDIPUS:

What a wicked old man you are! You'd try a stone's
Patience! Out with it! Have you no feeling at all?

TEIRESIAS:

You call me unfeeling. If you could only see
The nature of your own feelings . . .

OEDIPUS:

                                            Why,
Who would not feel as I do? Who could endure
Your arrogance toward the city?

TEIRESIAS:

What does it matter!
Whether I speak or not, it is bound to come.

OEDIPUS:

Then, if "it" is bound to come, you are bound to
tell me.

TEIRESIAS:

No, I will not go on. Rage as you please.

OEDIPUS:

Rage? Why not!
And I'll tell you what I think:
You planned it, you had it done, you all but
Killed him with your own hands: if you had eyes,
I'd say the crime was yours, and yours alone.

TEIRESIAS:

So? I charge you, then,
Abide by the proclamation you have made:
From this day forth
Never speak again to these men or to me;
You yourself are the pollution of this country.

OEDIPUS:

You dare say that! Can you possibly think you have
Some way of going free, after such insolence?

TEIRESIAS:

I have gone free. It is the truth sustains me.

OEDIPUS:

Who taught you shamelessness? It was not your craft.

TEIRESIAS:

You did. You made me speak. I did not want to.

OEDIPUS:

Speak what? Let me hear it again more clearly.

TEIRESIAS:

Was it not clear before? Are you tempting me?

OEDIPUS:

I did not understand it. Say it again.

TEIRESIAS:

I say that you are the murderer whom you seek.

OEDIPUS:

Now twice you have spat out infamy. You'll pay for
it!

TEIRESIAS:

Would you care for more? Do you wish to be really
angry?

OEDIPUS:

Say what you will. Whatever you say is worthless,

TEIRESIAS:

I say you live in hideous shame with those
Most dear to you. You can not see the evil.

OEDIPUS:

It seems you can go on mouthing like this for ever.

TEIRESIAS:

I can, if there is power in truth.

OEDIPUS:

There is:
But not for you, not for you,
You sightless, witless, senseless, mad old man!

TEIRESIAS:

You are the madman. There is no one here
Who will not curse you soon, as you curse me.

OEDIPUS:

You child of endless night! You can not hurt me
Or any other man who sees the sun.

TEIRESIAS:

True: it is not from me your fate will come.
That lies within Apollo's competence,
As it is his concern.

OEDIPUS:

Tell me:
Are you speaking for Creon, or for yourself?

TEIRESIAS:

Creon is no threat. You weave your own doom.

OEDIPUS:

Wealth, power, craft of statesmanship!
Kingly position, everywhere admired!
What savage envy is stored up against these,
If Creon, whom I trusted, Creon my friend,
For this great office which the city once
Put in my hands unsought—if for this power
Creon desires in secret to destroy me!

He has bought this decrepit fortune-teller, this
Collector of dirty pennies, this prophet fraud—
Why, he is no more clairvoyant than I am!
Tell us:
Has your mystic mummery ever approached the truth?
When that hellcat the Sphinx was performing here,
What help were you to these people?

Her magic was not for the first man who came along:
It demanded a real exorcist. Your birds—
What good were they? or the gods, for the matter of
    that?
But I came by,
Oedipus, the simple man, who knows nothing—
I thought it out for myself, no birds helped me!
And this is the man you think you can destroy,
That you may be close to Creon when he's king!
Well, you and your friend Creon, it seems to me,
Will suffer most. If you were not an old man,
You would have paid already for your plot.

CHORAGOS:

We can not see that his words or yours
Have been spoken except in anger, Oedipus,
And of anger we have no need. How can God's will
Be accomplished best? That is what most concerns
    us.

TEIRESIAS:

You are a king. But where argument's concerned
I am your man, as much a king as you.
I am not your servant, but Apollo's.
I have no need of Creon to speak for me.

Listen to me. You mock my blindness, do you?
But I say that you, with both your eyes, are blind:
You can not see the wretchedness of your life,
Nor in whose house you live, no, nor with whom.
Who are your father and mother? Can you tell me?
You do not even know the blind wrongs
That you have done them, on earth and in the world
    below.
But the double lash of your parents' curse will whip
    you
Out of this land some day, with only night

Upon your precious eyes.
Your cries then—where will they not be heard?
What fastness of Kithairon will not echo them?
And that bridal-descant of yours—you'll know it then,
The song they sang when you came here to Thebes
And found your misguided berthing.
All this, and more, that you can not guess at now,
Will bring you to yourself among your children.

Be angry, then. Curse Creon. Curse my words.
I tell you, no man that walks upon the earth
Shall be rooted out more horribly than you.

OEDIPUS:

Am I to bear this from him?—Damnation
Take you! Out of this place! Out of my sight!

TEIRESIAS:

I would not have come at all if you had not asked me.

OEDIPUS:

Could I have told that you'd talk nonsense, that
You'd come here to make a fool of yourself, and of
me?

TEIRESIAS:

A fool? Your parents thought me sane enough.

OEDIPUS:

My parents again!—Wait: who were my parents?

TEIRESIAS:

This day will give you a father, and break your heart.

OEDIPUS:

Your infantile riddles! Your damned abracadabra!

TEIRESIAS:

You were a great man once at solving riddles.

OEDIPUS:

Mock me with that if you like; you will find it true.

TEIRESIAS:

It was true enough. It brought about your ruin.

OEDIPUS:

But if it saved this town?

TEIRESIAS:

[*To the* PAGE:
Boy, give me your hand.

OEDIPUS:

Yes, boy; lead him away.
—While you are here
We can do nothing. Go; leave us in peace.

TEIRESIAS:

I will go when I have said what I have to say.
How can you hurt me? And I tell you again:
The man you have been looking for all this time,
The damned man, the murderer of Laïos,
That man is in Thebes. To your mind he is foreign-
born,
But it will soon be shown that he is a Theban,
A revelation that will fail to please.
A blind man,
Who has his eyes now; a penniless man, who is rich
now;
And he will go tapping the strange earth with his staff
To the children with whom he lives now he will be
Brother and father—the very same; to her
Who bore him, son and husband—the very same

Who came to his father's bed, wet with his father's
blood.

Enough. Go think that over.
If later you find error in what I have said,
You may say that I have no skill in prophecy.

> [*Exit* TEIRESIAS, *led by his* PAGE. OEDIPUS
> *goes into the palace.*

◆§ ODE I

CHORUS:

The Delphic stone of prophecies   [STROPHE 1
Remembers ancient regicide
And a still bloody hand.
That killer's hour of flight has come.
He must be stronger than riderless
Coursers of untiring wind,
For the son of Zeus armed with his father's thunder
Leaps in lightning after him;
And the Furies follow him, the sad Furies.

Holy Parnassos' peak of snow   [ANTISTROPHE 1
Flashes and blinds that secret man,
That all shall hunt him down:
Though he may roam the forest shade
Like a bull gone wild from pasture
To rage through glooms of stone.
Doom comes down on him; flight will not avail him;
For the world's heart calls him desolate,
And the immortal Furies follow, for ever follow.

But now a wilder thing is heard   [STROPHE 2
From the old man skilled at hearing Fate in the wing-
      beat of a bird.

Bewildered as a blown bird, my soul hovers and can
    not find
Foothold in this debate, or any reason or rest of mind.
But no man ever brought—none can bring
Proof of strife between Thebes' royal house,
Labdakos' line, and the son of Polybos;
And never until now has any man brought word
Of Laïos' dark death staining Oedipus the King.

Divine Zeus and Apollo hold   [ANTISTROPHE 2
Perfect intelligence alone of all tales ever told;
And well though this diviner works, he works in his
    own night;
No man can judge that rough unknown or trust in
    second sight,
For wisdom changes hands among the wise.
Shall I believe my great lord criminal
At a raging word that a blind old man let fall?
I saw him, when the carrion woman faced him of
    old,   *SPHINX*
Prove his heroic mind! These evil words are lies.

◄§ SCENE II

CREON:

    Men of Thebes:
    I am told that heavy accusations
    Have been brought against me by King Oedipus.

    I am not the kind of man to bear this tamely.

    If in these present difficulties
    He holds me accountable for any harm to him
    Through anything I have said or done—why, then,
    I do not value life in this dishonor.

It is not as though this rumor touched upon
Some private indiscretion. The matter is grave.
The fact is that I am being called disloyal
To the State, to my fellow citizens, to my friends.

CHORAGOS:

He may have spoken in anger, not from his mind.

CREON:

But did you not hear him say I was the one
Who seduced the old prophet into lying?

CHORAGOS:

The thing was said; I do not know how seriously.

CREON:

But you were watching him! Were his eyes steady?
Did he look like a man in his right mind?

CHORAGOS:

                           I do not know.
I can not judge the behavior of great men.
But here is the King himself.

                            [*Enter* OEDIPUS

OEDIPUS:

                        So you dared come back.
Why? How brazen of you to come to my house,
You murderer!
                   Do you think I do not know
That you plotted to kill me, plotted to steal my
      throne?
Tell me, in God's name: am I coward, a fool,
That you should dream you could accomplish this?
A fool who could not see your slippery game?
A coward, not to fight back when I saw it?
You are the fool, Creon, are you not? hoping

Without support or friends to get a throne?
Thrones may be won or bought: you could do neither.

CREON:

Now listen to me. You have talked; let me talk, too.
You can not judge unless you know the facts.

OEDIPUS:

You speak well: there is one fact; but I find it hard
To learn from the deadliest enemy I have.

CREON:

That above all I must dispute with you.

OEDIPUS:

That above all I will not hear you deny.

CREON·

If you think there is anything good in being stubborn
Against all reason, then I say you are wrong.

OEDIPUS:

If you think a man can sin against his own kind
And not be punished for it, I say you are mad.

CREON:

I agree. But tell me: what have I done to you?

OEDIPUS:

You advised me to send for that wizard, did you not?

CREON:

I did. I should do it again.

OEDIPUS:

           Very well. Now tell me:
How long has it been since Laïos—

CREON:

> What of Laïos?

OEDIPUS:

Since he vanished in that onset by the road?

CREON:

It was long ago, a long time.

OEDIPUS:

> And this prophet,
Was he practicing here then?

CREON:

> He was; and with honor, as now

OEDIPUS:

Did he speak of me at that time?

CREON:

> He never did;
At least, not when I was present.

OEDIPUS:

> But . . . the enquiry?
I suppose you held one?

CREON:

> We did, but we learned nothing.

OEDIPUS:

Why did the prophet not speak against me then?

CREON:

I do not know; and I am the kind of man
Who holds his tongue when he has no facts to go on.

OEDIPUS:

There's one fact that you know, and you could tell it.

CREON:

What fact is that? If I know it, you shall have it.

OEDIPUS:

If he were not involved with you, he could not say
That it was I who murdered Laïos.

CREON:

If he says that, you are the one that knows it!—
But now it is my turn to question you.

OEDIPUS:

Put your questions. I am no murderer.

CREON:

First, then: You married my sister?

OEDIPUS:

I married your sister.

CREON:

And you rule the kingdom equally with her?

OEDIPUS:

Everything that she wants she has from me.

CREON:

And I am the third, equal to both of you?

OEDIPUS:

That is why I call you a bad friend.

CREON:

No. Reason it out, as I have done.
Think of this first: Would any sane man prefer

Power, with all a king's anxieties,
To that same power and the grace of sleep?
Certainly not I.
I have never longed for the king's power—only his
    rights.
Would any wise man differ from me in this?
As matters stand, I have my way in everything
With your consent, and no responsibilities.
If I were king, I should be a slave to policy.

How could I desire a scepter more
Than what is now mine—untroubled influence?
No, I have not gone mad; I need no honors,
Except those with the perquisites I have now.
I am welcome everywhere; every man salutes me,
And those who want your favor seek my ear,
Since I know how to manage what they ask.
Should I exchange this ease for that anxiety?
Besides, no sober mind is treasonable.
I hate anarchy
And never would deal with any man who likes it.

Test what I have said. Go to the priestess
At Delphi, ask if I quoted her correctly.
And as for this other thing: if I am found
Guilty of treason with Teiresias,
Then sentence me to death! You have my word
It is a sentence I should cast my vote for—
But not without evidence!
                You do wrong
When you take good men for bad, bad men for good.
A true friend thrown aside—why, life itself
Is not more precious!
                In time you will know this well:
For time, and time alone, will show the just man,
Though scoundrels are discovered in a day.

CHORAGOS:

This is well said, and a prudent man would ponder it.
Judgments too quickly formed are dangerous.

OEDIPUS:

But is he not quick in his duplicity?
And shall I not be quick to parry him?
Would you have me stand still, hold my peace, and let
This man win everything, through my inaction?

CREON:

And you want—what is it, then? To banish me?

OEDIPUS:

No, not exile. It is your death I want,
So that all the world may see what treason means.

CREON:

You will persist, then? You will not believe me?

OEDIPUS:

How can I believe you?

CREON:

Then you are a fool.

OEDIPUS:

To save myself?

CREON:

In justice, think of me.

OEDIPUS:

You are evil incarnate.

CREON:

But suppose that you are wrong?

OEDIPUS:

Still I must rule.

CREON:

But not if you rule badly.

OEDIPUS:

O city, city!

CREON:

It is my city, too!

CHORAGOS:

Now, my lords, be still. I see the Queen,
Iocastê, coming from her palace chambers;
And it is time she came, for the sake of you both.
This dreadful quarrel can be resolved through her.

[*Enter* IOCASTE

IOCASTE:

Poor foolish men, what wicked din is this?
With Thebes sick to death, is it not shameful
That you should rake some private quarrel up?

[*To* OEDIPUS:

Come into the house.

—And you, Creon, go now:
Let us have no more of this tumult over nothing.

CREON:

Nothing? No, sister: what your husband plans for me
Is one of two great evils: exile or death.

OEDIPUS:

He is right.
Why, woman I have caught him squarely
Plotting against my life.

CREON:

No! Let me die
Accurst if ever I have wished you harm!

IOCASTE:

Ah, believe it, Oedipus!
In the name of the gods, respect this oath of his
For my sake, for the sake of these people here!

CHORAGOS: [STROPHE 1

Open your mind to her, my lord. Be ruled by her, I
     beg you!

OEDIPUS:

What would you have me do?

CHORAGOS:

Respect Creon's word. He has never spoken like a fool,
And now he has sworn an oath.

OEDIPUS:

You know what you ask?

CHORAGOS:

I do.

OEDIPUS:

Speak on, then.

CHORAGOS:

A friend so sworn should not be baited so,
In blind malice, and without final proof.

OEDIPUS:

You are aware, I hope, that what you say
Means death for me, or exile at the least.

CHORAGOS: [STROPHE 2

No, I swear by Helios, first in Heaven!
May I die friendless and accurst,
The worst of deaths, if ever I meant that!
It is the withering fields
That hurt my sick heart:
Must we bear all these ills,
And now your bad blood as well?

OEDIPUS:

Then let him go. And let me die, if I must,
Or be driven by him in shame from the land of
Thebes.
It is your unhappiness, and not his talk,
That touches me.
As for him—
Wherever he goes, hatred will follow him.

CREON:

Ugly in yielding, as you were ugly in rage!
Natures like yours chiefly torment themselves.

OEDIPUS:

Can you not go? Can you not leave me?

CREON:

I can.
You do not know me; but the city knows me,
And in its eyes I am just, if not in yours.

[Exit CREON

CHORAGOS: [ANTISTROPHE 1

Lady Iocastê, did you not ask the King to go to his
chambers?

IOCASTE:

First tell me what has happened.

CHORAGOS:

There was suspicion without evidence; yet it rankled
As even false charges will.

IOCASTE:

On both sides?

CHORAGOS:

On both.

IOCASTE:

But what was said?

CHORAGOS:

Oh let it rest, let it be done with!
Have we not suffered enough?

OEDIPUS:

You see to what your decency has brought you:
You have made difficulties where my heart saw none.

CHORAGOS: [ANTISTROPHE 2

Oedipus, it is not once only I have told you—
    You must know I should count myself unwise
To the point of madness, should I now forsake you—
        You, under whose hand,
            In the storm of another time,
        Our dear land sailed out free.
            But now stand fast at the helm!

IOCASTE:

In God's name, Oedipus, inform your wife as well:
Why are you so set in this hard anger?

OEDIPUS:

> I will tell you, for none of these men deserves
> My confidence as you do. It is Creon's work,
> His treachery, his plotting against me.

IOCASTE:

> Go on, if you can make this clear to me.

OEDIPUS:

> He charges me with the murder of Laïos.

IOCASTE:

> Has he some knowledge? Or does he speak from hearsay?

OEDIPUS:

> He would not commit himself to such a charge,
> But he has brought in that damnable soothsayer
> To tell his story.

IOCASTE:

>   Set your mind at rest.
> If it is a question of soothsayers, I tell you
> That you will find no man whose craft gives knowledge
> Of the unknowable.
>
>   Here is my proof:
>
> An oracle was reported to Laïos once
> (I will not say from Phoibos himself, but from
> His appointed ministers, at any rate)
> That his doom would be death at the hands of his
> own son—
> His son, born of his flesh and of mine!
>
> Now, you remember the story: Laïos was killed

By marauding strangers where three highways meet;
But his child had not been three days in this world
Before the King had pierced the baby's ankles
And left him to die on a lonely mountainside.

Thus, Apollo never caused that child
To kill his father, and it was not Laïos' fate
To die at the hands of his son, as he had feared.
This is what prophets and prophecies are worth!
Have no dread of them.
                              It is God himself
Who can show us what he wills, in his own way.

OEDIPUS:

How strange a shadowy memory crossed my mind,
Just now while you were speaking; it chilled my heart .

IOCASTE:

What do you mean? What memory do you speak of?

OEDIPUS:

If I understand you, Laïos was killed
At a place where three roads meet.

IOCASTE:

                              So it was said;
We have no later story.

OEDIPUS:

                    Where did it happen?

IOCASTE:

Phokis, it is called: at a place where the Theban Way
Divides into the roads toward Delphi and Daulia.

OEDIPUS:

When?

IOCASTE:

> We had the news not long before you came
> And proved the right to your succession here.

OEDIPUS:

Ah, what net has God been weaving for me?

IOCASTE:

Oedipus! Why does this trouble you?

OEDIPUS:

> > > > > Do not ask me yet.
> First, tell me how Laïos looked, and tell me
> How old he was.

IOCASTE:

> > > > He was tall, his hair just touched
> With white; his form was not unlike your own.

OEDIPUS:

> I think that I myself may be accurst
> By my own ignorant edict.

IOCASTE:

> > > > You speak strangely.
> It makes me tremble to look at you, my King.

OEDIPUS:

> I am not sure that the blind man can not see.
> But I should know better if you were to tell me—

IOCASTE:

Anything—though I dread to hear you ask it.

OEDIPUS:

> Was the King lightly escorted, or did he ride
> With a large company, as a ruler should?

IOCASTE:

There were five men with him in all: one was a herald,
And a single chariot, which he was driving.

OEDIPUS:

Alas, that makes it plain enough!
                                    But who—
Who told you how it happened?

IOCASTE:

                            A household servant,
The only one to escape.

OEDIPUS:

                    And is he still
A servant of ours?

IOCASTE:

                    No; for when he came back at last
And found you enthroned in the place of the dead
      king,
He came to me, touched my hand with his, and
      begged
That I would send him away to the frontier district
Where only the shepherds go—
As far away from the city as I could send him.
I granted his prayer; for although the man was a slave,
He had earned more than this favor at my hands.

OEDIPUS:

Can he be called back quickly?

IOCASTE:

                                Easily.
But why?

OEDIPUS:

> I have taken too much upon myself
> Without enquiry; therefore I wish to consult him.

IOCASTE:

> Then he shall come.
>   But am I not one also
> To whom you might confide these fears of yours?

OEDIPUS:

> That is your right; it will not be denied you,
> Now least of all; for I have reached a pitch
> Of wild foreboding. Is there anyone
> To whom I should sooner speak?
>
> Polybos of Corinth is my father.
> My mother is a Dorian: Meropê.
> I grew up chief among the men of Corinth
> Until a strange thing happened—
> Not worth my passion, it may be, but strange.
>
> At a feast, a drunken man maundering in his cups
> Cries out that I am not my father's son!
>
> I contained myself that night, though I felt anger
> And a sinking heart. The next day I visited
> My father and mother, and questioned them. They
>   stormed,
> Calling it all the slanderous rant of a fool;
> And this relieved me. Yet the suspicion
> Remained always aching in my mind;
> I knew there was talk; I could not rest;
> And finally, saying nothing to my parents,
> I went to the shrine at Delphi.

The god dismissed my question without reply;
He spoke of other things.
                                    Some were clear,
Full of wretchedness, dreadful, unbearable:
As, that I should lie with my own mother, breed
Children from whom all men would turn their eyes;
And that I should be my father's murderer.

I heard all this, and fled. And from that day
Corinth to me was only in the stars
Descending in that quarter of the sky,
As I wandered farther and farther on my way
To a land where I should never see the evil
Sung by the oracle. And I came to this country
Where, so you say, King Laïos was killed.

I will tell you all that happened there, my lady.

There were three highways
Coming together at a place I passed;
And there a herald came towards me, and a chariot
Drawn by horses, with a man such as you describe
Seated in it. The groom leading the horses
Forced me off the road at his lord's command;
But as this charioteer lurched over towards me
I struck him in my rage. The old man saw me
And brought his double goad down upon my head
As I came abreast.
                        He was paid back, and more!
Swinging my club in this right hand I knocked him
Out of his car, and he rolled on the ground.
                                    I killed him.

I killed them all.
Now if that stranger and Laïos were—kin,
Where is a man more miserable than I?

More hated by the gods? Citizen and alien alike
Must never shelter me or speak to me—
I must be shunned by all.

                            And I myself
Pronounced this malediction upon myself!

Think of it: I have touched you with these hands,
These hands that killed your husband. What defile-
    ment!

Am I all evil, then? It must be so,
Since I must flee from Thebes, yet never again
See my own countrymen, my own country,
For fear of joining my mother in marriage
And killing Polybos, my father.

                             Ah,
If I was created so, born to this fate,
Who could deny the savagery of God?

O holy majesty of heavenly powers!
May I never see that day! Never!
Rather let me vanish from the race of men
Than know the abomination destined me!

CHORAGOS:

We too, my lord, have felt dismay at this.
But there is hope: you have yet to hear the shepherd.

OEDIPUS:

Indeed, I fear no other hope is left me.

IOCASTE:

What do you hope from him when he comes?

OEDIPUS:

                             This much:
If his account of the murder tallies with yours,
Then I am cleared.

IOCASTE:

What was it that I said
Of such importance?

OEDIPUS:

Why, "marauders," you said,
Killed the King, according to this man's story.
If he maintains that still, if there were several,
Clearly the guilt is not mine: I was alone.
But if he says one man, singlehanded, did it,
Then the evidence all points to me.

IOCASTE:

You may be sure that he said there were several;
And can he call back that story now? He cán not.
The whole city heard it as plainly as I.
But suppose he alters some detail of it:
He can not ever show that Laïos' death
Fulfilled the oracle: for Apollo said
My child was doomed to kill him; and my child—
Poor baby!—it was my child that died first.

No. From now on, where oracles are concerned,
I would not waste a second thought on any.

OEDIPUS:

You may be right.
But come: let someone go
For the shepherd at once. This matter must be settled.

IOCASTE:

I will send for him.
I would not wish to cross you in anything,
And surely not in this.—Let us go in.
                              [Exeunt into the palace

ODE II

CHORUS: [STROPHE 1

Let me be reverent in the ways of right,
Lowly the paths I journey on;
Let all my words and actions keep
The laws of the pure universe
From highest Heaven handed down.
For Heaven is their bright nurse,
Those generations of the realms of light;
Ah, never of mortal kind were they begot,
Nor are they slaves of memory, lost in sleep:
Their Father is greater than Time, and ages not.

The tyrant is a child of Pride [ANTISTROPHE 1
Who drinks from his great sickening cup
Recklessness and vanity,
Until from his high crest headlong
He plummets to the dust of hope.
That strong man is not strong.
But let no fair ambition be denied;
May God protect the wrestler for the State
In government, in comely policy,
Who will fear God, and on His ordinance wait.

[STROPHE 2

Haughtiness and the high hand of disdain
Tempt and outrage God's holy law;
And any mortal who dares hold
No immortal Power in awe
Will be caught up in a net of pain:
The price for which his levity is sold.
Let each man take due earnings, then,
And keep his hands from holy things,

And from blasphemy stand apart—
Else the crackling blast of heaven
Blows on his head, and on his desperate heart;
Though fools will honor impious men,
In their cities no tragic poet sings.

[ANTISTROPHE 2

Shall we lose faith in Delphi's obscurities,
We who have heard the world's core
Discredited, and the sacred wood
Of Zeus at Elis praised no more?
The deeds and the strange prophecies
Must make a pattern yet to be understood.
Zeus, if indeed you are lord of all,
Throned in light over night and day,
Mirror this in your endless mind:
Our masters call the oracle
Words on the wind, and the Delphic vision blind!
Their hearts no longer know Apollo,
And reverence for the gods has died away.

•§ SCENE III

[Enter IOCASTE

IOCASTE:

Princes of Thebes, it has occurred to me
To visit the altars of the gods, bearing
These branches as a suppliant, and this incense.
Our King is not himself: his noble soul
Is overwrought with fantasies of dread,
Else he would consider
The new prophecies in the light of the old.
He will listen to any voice that speaks disaster,
And my advice goes for nothing.

[She approaches the altar, R.

To you, then, Apollo,
Lycean lord, since you are nearest, I turn in prayer.

Receive these offerings, and grant us deliverance
From defilement. Our hearts are heavy with fear
When we see our leader distracted, as helpless sailors
Are terrified by the confusion of their helmsman.

[*Enter* MESSENGER

MESSENGER:

Friends, no doubt you can direct me:
Where shall I find the house of Oedipus,
Or, better still, where is the King himself?

CHORAGOS:

It is this very place, stranger; he is inside.
This is his wife and mother of his children.

MESSENGER:

I wish her happiness in a happy house,
Blest in all the fulfillment of her marriage.

IOCASTE:

I wish as much for you: your courtesy
Deserves a like good fortune. But now, tell me:
Why have you come? What have you to say to us?

MESSENGER:

Good news, my lady, for your house and your husband.

IOCASTE:

What news? Who sent you here?

MESSENGER:

I am from Corinth.
The news I bring ought to mean joy for you,
Though it may be you will find some grief in it.

IOCASTE:

What is it? How can it touch us in both ways?

MESSENGER:

The word is that the people of the Isthmus
Intend to call Oedipus to be their king.

IOCASTE:

But old King Polybos—is he not reigning still?

MESSENGER:

No. Death holds him in his sepulchre.

IOCASTE:

What are you saying? Polybos is dead?

MESSENGER:

If I am not telling the truth, may I die myself.

IOCASTE: [To a MAIDSERVANT:

Go in, go quickly; tell this to your master.

O riddlers of God's will, where are you now!
This was the man whom Oedipus, long ago,
Feared so, fled so, in dread of destroying him—
But it was another fate by which he died.
[Enter OEDIPUS, C.

OEDIPUS:

Dearest Iocastê, why have you sent for me?

IOCASTE:

Listen to what this man says, and then tell me
What has become of the solemn prophecies.

OEDIPUS:

Who is this man? What is his news for me?

IOCASTE:

He has come from Corinth to announce your father's
death!

OEDIPUS:

Is it true, stranger? Tell me in your own words.

MESSENGER:

I can not say it more clearly: the King is dead.

OEDIPUS:

Was it by treason? Or by an attack of illness?

MESSENGER:

A little thing brings old men to their rest.

OEDIPUS:

It was sickness, then?

MESSENGER:

Yes, and his many years.

OEDIPUS:

Ah!
Why should a man respect the Pythian hearth, or
Give heed to the birds that jangle above his head?
They prophesied that I should kill Polybos,
Kill my own father; but he is dead and buried,
And I am here—I never touched him, never,
Unless he died of grief for my departure,
And thus, in a sense, through me. No. Polybos
Has packed the oracles off with him underground.
They are empty words.

IOCASTE:

Had I not told you so?

OEDIPUS:

You had; it was my faint heart that betrayed me.

IOCASTE:

From now on never think of those things again

OEDIPUS:

And yet—must I not fear my mother's bed?

IOCASTE:

Why should anyone in this world be afraid,
Since Fate rules us and nothing can be foreseen?
A man should live only for the present day.

Have no more fear of sleeping with your mother:
How many men, in dreams, have lain with their
        mothers!
No reasonable man is troubled by such things.

OEDIPUS:

That is true; only—
If only my mother were not still alive!
But she is alive. I can not help my dread.

IOCASTE:

Yet this news of your father's death is wonderful.

OEDIPUS:

Wonderful. But I fear the living woman.

MESSENGER:

Tell me, who is this woman that you fear?

OEDIPUS:

It is Meropê, man; the wife of King Polybos.

MESSENGER:

Meropê? Why should you be afraid of her?

OEDIPUS:

An oracle of the gods, a dreadful saying.

MESSENGER:

Can you tell me about it or are you sworn to silence?

OEDIPUS:

I can tell you, and I will.
Apollo said through his prophet that I was the man
Who should marry his own mother, shed his father's
    blood
With his own hands. And so, for all these years
I have kept clear of Corinth, and no harm has come—
Though it would have been sweet to see my parents
    again.

MESSENGER:

And is this the fear that drove you out of Corinth?

OEDIPUS:

Would you have me kill my father?

MESSENGER:

                                    As for that
You must be reassured by the news I gave you.

OEDIPUS:

If you could reassure me, I would reward you.

MESSENGER:

I had that in mind, I will confess: I thought
I could count on you when you returned to Corinth.

OEDIPUS:

No: I will never go near my parents again.

MESSENGER:

Ah, son, you still do not know what you are doing—

OEDIPUS:

What do you mean? In the name of God tell me!

MESSENGER:

—If these are your reasons for not going home.

OEDIPUS:

I tell you, I fear the oracle may come true.

MESSENGER:

And guilt may come upon you through your parents?

OEDIPUS:

That is the dread that is always in my heart.

MESSENGER:

Can you not see that all your fears are groundless?

OEDIPUS:

How can you say that? They are my parents, surely?

MESSENGER:

Polybos was not your father.

OEDIPUS:

Not my father?

MESSENGER:

No more your father than the man speaking to you.

OEDIPUS:

But you are nothing to me!

MESSENGER:

Neither was he.

OEDIPUS:

Then why did he call me son?

MESSENGER:

I will tell you:
Long ago he had you from my hands, as a gift.

OEDIPUS:

Then how could he love me so, if I was not his?

MESSENGER:

He had no children, and his heart turned to you.

OEDIPUS:

What of you? Did you buy me? Did you find me by
chance?

MESSENGER:

I came upon you in the crooked pass of Kithairon.

OEDIPUS:

And what were you doing there?

MESSENGER:

Tending my flocks.

OEDIPUS:

A wandering shepherd?

MESSENGER:

But your savior, son, that day.

OEDIPUS:

From what did you save me?

MESSENGER:

Your ankles should tell you that.

OEDIPUS:

Ah, stranger, why do you speak of that childhood pain?

MESSENGER:

I cut the bonds that tied your ankles together.

OEDIPUS:

I have had the mark as long as I can remember.

MESSENGER:

That was why you were given the name you bear.

OEDIPUS:

God! Was it my father or my mother who did it? Tell me!

MESSENGER:

I do not know. The man who gave you to me Can tell you better than I.

OEDIPUS:

It was not you that found me, but another?

MESSENGER:

It was another shepherd gave you to me.

OEDIPUS:

Who was he? Can you tell me who he was?

MESSENGER:

I think he was said to be one of Laïos' people.

OEDIPUS:

You mean the Laïos who was king here years ago?

MESSENGER:

Yes; King Laïos; and the man was one of his herds-
men.

OEDIPUS:

Is he still alive? Can I see him?

MESSENGER:

These men here
Know best about such things.

OEDIPUS:

Does anyone here
Know this shepherd that he is talking about?
Have you seen him in the fields, or in the town?
If you have, tell me. It is time things were made plain.

CHORAGOS:

I think the man he means is that same shepherd
You have already asked to see. Iocastê perhaps
Could tell you something.

OEDIPUS:

Do you know anything
About him, Lady? Is he the man we have summoned?
Is that the man this shepherd means?

IOCASTE:

Why think of him?
Forget this herdsman. Forget it all.
This talk is a waste of time.

OEDIPUS:

How can you say that,
When the clues to my true birth are in my hands?

IOCASTE:

For God's love, let us have no more questioning!
Is your life nothing to you?
My own is pain enough for me to bear.

OEDIPUS:

You need not worry. Suppose my mother a slave,
And born of slaves: no baseness can touch you.

IOCASTE:

Listen to me, I beg you: do not do this thing!

OEDIPUS:

I will not listen; the truth must be made known.

IOCASTE:

Everything that I say is for your own good!

OEDIPUS:

My own good
Snaps my patience, then; I want none of it.

IOCASTE:

You are fatally wrong! May you never learn who you
are!

OEDIPUS:

Go, one of you, and bring the shepherd here.
Let us leave this woman to brag of her royal name.

IOCASTE:

Ah, miserable!
That is the only word I have for you now.
That is the only word I can ever have.

[*Exit into the palace*

CHORAGOS:

Why has she left us, Oedipus? Why has she gone
In such a passion of sorrow? I fear this silence:
Something dreadful may come of it.

OEDIPUS:

Let it come!
However base my birth, I must know about it.
The Queen, like a woman, is perhaps ashamed
To think of my low origin. But I
Am a child of Luck; I can not be dishonored.
Luck is my mother; the passing months, my brothers,
Have seen me rich and poor.
If this is so,
How could I wish that I were someone else?
How could I not be glad to know my birth?

◄§ ODE III

CHORUS:

If ever the coming time were known   [STROPHE
To my heart's pondering,
Kithairon, now by Heaven I see the torches
At the festival of the next full moon,
And see the dance, and hear the choir sing
A grace to your gentle shade:
Mountain where Oedipus was found,
O mountain guard of a noble race!

May the god who heals us lend his aid,
And let that glory come to pass
For our king's cradling-ground.

[ANTISTROPHE

Of the nymphs that flower beyond the years,
Who bore you, royal child,
To Pan of the hills or the timberline Apollo,
Cold in delight where the upland clears,
Or Hermês for whom Kyllenê's heights are piled?
Or flushed as evening cloud,
Great Dionysos, roamer of mountains,
He—was it he who found you there,
And caught you up in his own proud
Arms from the sweet god-ravisher
Who laughed by the Muses' fountains?

◆§ SCENE IV

OEDIPUS:

Sirs: though I do not know the man,
I think I see him coming, this shepherd we want:
He is old, like our friend here, and the men
Bringing him seem to be servants of my house.
But you can tell, if you have ever seen him.
[Enter SHEPHERD escorted by servants

CHORAGOS:

I know him, he was Laïos' man. You can trust him.

OEDIPUS:

Tell me first, you from Corinth: is this the shepherd
We were discussing?

MESSENGER:

This is the very man.

OEDIPUS: [*To* SHEPHERD

Come here. No, look at me. You must answer
Everything I ask.—You belonged to Laïos?

SHEPHERD:

Yes: born his slave, brought up in his house.

OEDIPUS:

Tell me: what kind of work did you do for him?

SHEPHERD:

I was a shepherd of his, most of my life.

OEDIPUS:

Where mainly did you go for pasturage?

SHEPHERD:

Sometimes Kithairon, sometimes the hills near-by.

OEDIPUS:

Do you remember ever seeing this man out there?

SHEPHERD:

What would he be doing there? This man?

OEDIPUS:

This man standing here. Have you ever seen him
before?

SHEPHERD:

No. At least, not to my recollection.

MESSENGER:

> And that is not strange, my lord. But I'll refresh
> His memory: he must remember when we two
> Spent three whole seasons together, March to Septem-
> ber,
> On Kithairon or thereabouts. He had two flocks;
> I had one. Each autumn I'd drive mine home
> And he would go back with his to Laïos' sheepfold.—
> Is this not true, just as I have described it?

SHEPHERD:

> True, yes; but it was all so long ago.

MESSENGER:

> Well, then: do you remember, back in those days,
> That you gave me a baby boy to bring up as my own?

SHEPHERD:

> What if I did? What are you trying to say?

MESSENGER:

> King Oedipus was once that little child.

SHEPHERD:

> Damn you, hold your tongue!

OEDIPUS:

> No more of that!
> It is your tongue needs watching, not this man's.

SHEPHERD:

> My King, my Master, what is it I have done wrong?

OEDIPUS:

> You have not answered his question about the boy.

SHEPHERD:

Он does not know . . . He is only making trouble . . .

OEDIPUS:

Come, speak plainly, or it will go hard with you.

SHEPHERD:

In God's name, do not torture an old man!

OEDIPUS:

Come here, one of you; bind his arms behind him.

SHEPHERD:

Unhappy king! What more do you wish to learn?

OEDIPUS:

Did you give this man the child he speaks of?

SHEPHERD:

I did.

And I would to God I had died that very day.

OEDIPUS:

You will die now unless you speak the truth.

SHEPHERD:

Yet if I speak the truth, I am worse than dead.

OEDIPUS:

Very well; since you insist upon delaying—

SHEPHERD:

No! I have told you already that I gave him the boy.

OEDIPUS:

Where did you get him? From your house? From
somewhere else?

SHEPHERD:

Not from mine, no. A man gave him to me.

OEDIPUS:

Is that man here? Do you know whose slave he was?

SHEPHERD:

For God's love, my King, do not ask me any more!

OEDIPUS:

You are a dead man if I have to ask you again.

SHEPHERD:

Then . . . Then the child was from the palace of
Laïos.

OEDIPUS:

A slave child? or a child of his own line?

SHEPHERD:

Ah, I am on the brink of dreadful speech!

OEDIPUS:

And I of dreadful hearing. Yet I must hear.

SHEPHERD:

If you must be told, then . . .
                              They said it was Laïos' child;
But it is your wife who can tell you about that.

OEDIPUS:

My wife!—Did she give it to you?

SHEPHERD:

                              My lord, she did.

OEDIPUS:

Do you know why?

SHEPHERD:

I was told to get rid of it.

OEDIPUS:

An unspeakable mother!

SHEPHERD:

There had been prophecies . . .

OEDIPUS:

Tell me.

SHEPHERD:

It was said that the boy would kill his own father.

OEDIPUS:

Then why did you give him over to this old man?

SHEPHERD:

I pitied the baby, my King,
And I thought that this man would take him far away
To his own country.
                    He saved him—but for what a fate!
For if you are what this man says you are,
No man living is more wretched than Oedipus.

OEDIPUS:

Ah God!
It was true!
            All the prophecies!
                                —Now,
O Light, may I look on you for the last time!
I, Oedipus,

Oedipus, damned in his birth, in his marriage damned,
Damned in the blood he shed with his own hand!
                    [*He rushes into the palace*

◄§ ODE IV

CHORUS:

Alas for the seed of men.   [STROPHE 1

What measure shall I give these generations
That breathe on the void and are void
And exist and do not exist?

Who bears more weight of joy
Than mass of sunlight shifting in images,
Or who shall make his thought stay on
That down time drifts away?

Your splendor is all fallen.

O naked brow of wrath and tears,
O change of Oedipus!
I who saw your days call no man blest—
Your great days like ghósts góne.

That mind was a strong bow.   [ANTISTROPHE 1

Deep, how deep you drew it then, hard archer,
At a dim fearful range,
And brought dear glory down!

You overcame the stranger—
The virgin with her hooking lion claws—

And though death sang, stood like a tower
To make pale Thebes take heart.

Fortress against our sorrow!

True king, giver of laws,
Majestic Oedipus!
No prince in Thebes had ever such renown,
No prince won such grace of power.

And now of all men ever known   [STROPHE 2
Most pitiful is this man's story:
His fortunes are most changed, his state
Fallen to a low slave's
Ground under bitter fate.

O Oedipus, most royal one!
The great door that expelled you to the light
Gave at night—ah, gave night to your glory:
As to the father, to the fathering son.

All understood too late.

How could that queen whom Laïos won,
The garden that he harrowed at his height,
Be silent when that act was done?

But all eyes fail before time's eye,   [ANTISTROPHE 2
All actions come to justice there.
Though never willed, though far down the deep past,
Your bed, your dread sirings,
Are brought to book at last.

Child by Laïos doomed to die,
Then doomed to lose that fortunate little death,
Would God you never took breath in this air
That with my wailing lips I take to cry:

For I weep the world's outcast.

I was blind, and now I can tell why:
Asleep, for you had given ease of breath
To Thebes, while the false years went by.

◆§ ÉXODOS

[*Enter, from the palace,* SECOND MESSENGER

SECOND MESSENGER:

Elders of Thebes, most honored in this land,
What horrors are yours to see and hear, what weight
Of sorrow to be endured, if, true to your birth,
You venerate the line of Labdakos!
I think neither Istros nor Phasis, those great rivers,
Could purify this place of the corruption
It shelters now, or soon must bring to light—
Evil not done unconsciously, but willed.

The greatest griefs are those we cause ourselves.

CHORAGOS:

Surely, friend, we have grief enough already;
What new sorrow do you mean?

'COND MESSENGER:

                              The Queen is dead.

CHORAGOS:

Iocastê? Dead? But at whose hand?

SECOND MESSENGER:

Her own.
The full horror of what happened you can not know,
For you did not see it; but I, who did, will tell you
As clearly as I can how she met her death.

When she had left us,
In passionate silence, passing through the court,
She ran to her apartment in the house,
Her hair clutched by the fingers of both hands.
She closed the doors behind her; then, by that bed
Where long ago the fatal son was conceived—
That son who should bring about his father's death—
We heard her call upon Laïos, dead so many years,
And heard her wail for the double fruit of her mar-
    riage,
A husband by her husband, children by her child.

Exactly how she died I do not know:
For Oedipus burst in moaning and would not let us
Keep vigil to the end: it was by him
As he stormed about the room that our eyes were
    caught.
From one to another of us he went, begging a sword,
Cursing the wife who was not his wife, the mother
Whose womb had carried his own children and him-
    self.
I do not know: it was none of us aided him,
But surely one of the gods was in control!
For with a dreadful cry
He hurled his weight, as though wrenched out of him-
    self,
At the twin doors: the bolts gave, and he rushed in.

And there we saw her hanging, her body swaying
From the cruel cord she had noosed about her neck.
A great sob broke from him, heartbreaking to hear,
As he loosed the rope and lowered her to the ground.

I would blot out from my mind what happened next!
For the King ripped from her gown the golden
        brooches
That were her ornament, and raised them, and
        plunged them down
Straight into his own eyeballs, crying, "No more,
No more shall you look on the misery about me,
The horrors of my own doing! Too long you have
        known
The faces of those whom I should never have seen,
Too long been blind to those for whom I was search-
        ing!
From this hour, go in darkness!" And as he spoke,
He struck at his eyes—not once, but many times;
And the blood spattered his beard,
Bursting from his ruined sockets like red hail.

So from the unhappiness of two this evil has sprung,
A curse on the man and woman alike. The old
Happiness of the house of Labdakos
Was happiness enough: where is it today?
It is all wailing and ruin, disgrace, death—all
The misery of mankind that has a name—
And it is wholly and for ever theirs.

CHORAGOS:

Is he in agony still? Is there no rest for him?

SECOND MESSENGER:

He is calling for someone to lead him to the gates
So that all the children of Kadmos may look upon
His father's murderer, his mother's—no,

I can not say it!
                    And then he will leave Thebes,
Self-exiled, in order that the curse
Which he himself pronounced may depart from the
    house.
He is weak, and there is none to lead him,
So terrible is his suffering.
                        But you will see:
Look, the doors are opening; in a moment
You will see a thing that would crush a heart of stone.
            [*The central door is opened;* OEDIPUS,
            blinded, is led in

CHORAGOS:

Dreadful indeed for men to see.
Never have my own eyes
Looked on a sight so full of fear.

Oedipus!
What madness came upon you, what daemon
Leaped on your life with heavier
Punishment than a mortal man can bear?
No: I can not even
Look at you, poor ruined one.
And I would speak, question, ponder,
If I were able. No.
You make me shudder.

OEDIPUS:

God.   God.
Is there a sorrow greater?
Where shall I find harbor in this world?
My voice is hurled far on a dark wind.
What has God done to me?

CHORAGOS:

Too terrible to think of, or to see.

OEDIPUS:

O cloud of night,   [STROPHE 1
Never to be turned away: night coming on,
I can not tell how: night like a shroud!

My fair winds brought me here.
                              O God. Again
The pain of the spikes where I had sight,
The flooding pain
Of memory, never to be gouged out.

CHORAGOS:

This is not strange.
You suffer it all twice over, remorse in pain,
Pain in remorse.

OEDIPUS:

Ah dear friend   [ANTISTROPHE 1
Are you faithful even yet, you alone?
Are you still standing near me, will you stay here,
Patient, to care for the blind?
                              The blind man!
Yet even blind I know who it is attends me,
By the voice's tone—
Though my new darkness hide the comforter.

CHORAGOS:

Oh fearful act!
What god was it drove you to rake black
Night across your eyes?

OEDIPUS:

Apollo. Apollo. Dear   [STROPHE 2
Children, the god was Apollo.

He brought my sick, sick fate upon me.
But the blinding hand was mv own!
How could I bear to see
When all my sight was horror everywhere?

CHORAGOS:

Everywhere; that is true.

OEDIPUS:

And now what is left?
Images? Love? A greeting even,
Sweet to the senses? Is there anything?
Ah, no, friends: lead me away.
Lead me away from Thebes.
                                 Lead the great wreck
And hell of Oedipus, whom the gods hate.

CHORAGOS:

Your fate is clear, you are not blind to that.
Would God you had never found it out!

OEDIPUS: [ANTISTROPHE 2

Death take the man who unbound
My feet on that hillside
And delivered me from death to life! What life?
If only I had died,
This weight of monstrous doom
Could not have dragged me and my darlings down.

CHORAGOS:

I would have wished the same.

OEDIPUS:

Oh never to have come here
With my father's blood upon me! Never
To have been the man they call his mother's hus-
    band!

Oh accurst! Oh child of evil,
To have entered that wretched bed—
                    the selfsame one!
More primal than sin itself, this fell to me.

CHORAGOS:

I do not know how I can answer you.
You were better dead than alive and blind.

OEDIPUS:

Do not counsel me any more. This punishment
That I have laid upon myself is just.
If I had eyes,
I do not know how I could bear the sight
Of my father, when I came to the house of Death,
Or my mother: for I have sinned against them both
So vilely that I could not make my peace
By strangling my own life.
                  Or do you think my children,
Born as they were born, would be sweet to my eyes?
Ah never, never! Nor this town with its high walls,
Nor the holy images of the gods.
               For I,
Thrice miserable!—Oedipus, noblest of all the line
Of Kadmos, have condemned myself to enjoy
These things no more, by my own malediction
Expelling that man whom the gods declared
To be a defilement in the house of Laïos.
After exposing the rankness of my own guilt,
How could I look men frankly in the eyes?
No, I swear it,
If I could have stifled my hearing at its source,
I would have done it and made all this body
A tight cell of misery, blank to light and sound:
So I should have been safe in a dark agony
Beyond all recollection.
             Ah Kithairon!

Why did you shelter me? When I was cast upon you,
Why did I not die? Then I should never
Have shown the world my execrable birth.

Ah Polybos! Corinth, city that I believed
The ancient seat of my ancestors: how fair
I seemed, your child! And all the while this evil
Was cancerous within me!
                      For I am sick
In my daily life, sick in my origin.

O three roads, dark ravine, woodland and way
Where three roads met: you, drinking my father's
    blood,
My own blood, spilled by my own hand: can you
    remember
The unspeakable things I did there, and the things
I went on from there to do?
                   O marriage, marriage!
The act that engendered me, and again the act
Performed by the son in the same bed—
                        Ah, the net
Of incest, mingling fathers, brothers, sons,
With brides, wives, mothers: the last evil
That can be known by men: no tongue can say
How evil!
         No. For the love of God, conceal me
Somewhere far from Thebes; or kill me; or hurl me
Into the sea, away from men's eyes for ever.

Come, lead me. You need not fear to touch me.
Of all men, I alone can bear this guilt.

                            [*Enter* CREON

CHORAGOS:

We are not the ones to decide; but Creon here
May fitly judge of what you ask. He only
Is left to protect the city in your place.

OEDIPUS:

Alas, how can I speak to him? What right have I
To beg his courtesy whom I have deeply wronged?

CREON:

I have not come to mock you, Oedipus,
Or to reproach you, either.

[TO ATTENDANTS:
—You, standing there:
If you have lost all respect for man's dignity,
At least respect the flame of Lord Helios:
Do not allow this pollution to show itself
Openly here, an affront to the earth
And Heaven's rain and the light of day. No, take him
Into the house as quickly as you can.
For it is proper
That only the close kindred see his grief.

OEDIPUS:

I pray you in God's name, since your courtesy
Ignores my dark expectation, visiting
With mercy this man of all men most execrable:
Give me what I ask—for your good, not for mine.

CREON:

And what is it that you would have me do?

OEDIPUS:

Drive me out of this country as quickly as may be
To a place where no human voice can ever greet me.

CREON:

I should have done that before now—only,
God's will had not been wholly revealed to me.

OEDIPUS:

But his command is plain: the parricide
Must be destroyed. I am that evil man.

CREON:

That is the sense of it, yes; but as things are,
We had best discover clearly what is to be done.

OEDIPUS:

You would learn more about a man like me?

CREON:

You are ready now to listen to the god.

OEDIPUS:

I will listen. But it is to you
That I must turn for help. I beg you, hear me.

The woman in there—
Give her whatever funeral you think proper:
She is your sister.
                 —But let me go, Creon!
Let me purge my father's Thebes of the pollution
Of my living here, and go out to the wild hills,
To Kithairon, that has won such fame with me,
The tomb my mother and father appointed for me,
And let me die there, as they willed I should.
And yet I know
Death will not ever come to me through sickness
Or in any natural way: I have been preserved
For some unthinkable fate. But let that be.

As for my sons, you need not care for them.
They are men, they will find some way to live.
But my poor daughters, who have shared my table,
Who never before have been parted from their
    father—
Take care of them, Creon; do this for me.

And will you let me touch them with my hands
A last time, and let us weep together?
Be kind, my lord,
Great prince, be kind!
                    Could I but touch them,
They would be mine again, as when I had my eyes.
                    [Enter ANTIGONE and ISMENE, attended
Ah, God!
Is it my dearest children I hear weeping?
Has Creon pitied me and sent my daughters?

CREON:

Yes, Oedipus: I knew that they were dear to you
In the old days, and know you must love them still.

OEDIPUS:

May God bless you for this—and be a friendlier
Guardian to you than he has been to me!

Children, where are you?
Come quickly to my hands: they are your brother's—
Hands that have brought your father's once clear eyes
To this way of seeing—
                    Ah dearest ones,
I had neither sight nor knowledge then, your father
By the woman who was the source of his own life!
And I weep for you—having no strength to see you—,
I weep for you when I think of the bitterness
That men will visit upon you all your lives.
What homes, what festivals can you attend
Without being forced to depart again in tears?
And when you come to marriageable age,
Where is the man, my daughters, who would dare
Risk the bane that lies on all my children?
Is there any evil wanting? Your father killed
His father; sowed the womb of her who bore him;
Engendered you at the fount of his own existence!

That is what they will say of you.

                         Then, whom
Can you ever marry? There are no bridegrooms for
    you,
And your lives must wither away in sterile dreaming.

O Creon, son of Menoikeus!
You are the only father my daughters have,
Since we, their parents, are both of us gone for ever.
They are your own blood: you will not let them
Fall into beggary and loneliness;
You will keep them from the miseries that are mine!
Take pity on them; see, they are only children,
Friendless except for you. Promise me this,
Great Prince, and give me your hand in token of it.
                   [CREON *clasps his right hand*

Children:
I could say much, if you could understand me,
But as it is, I have only this prayer for you:
Live where you can, be as happy as you can—
Happier, please God, than God has made your father!

CREON:

Enough. You have wept enough. Now go within.

OEDIPUS:

I must; but it is hard.

CREON:

                     Time eases all things.

OEDIPUS:

But you must promise—

CREON:

                     Say what you desire.

OEDIPUS:

Send me from Thebes!

CREON:

God grant that I may!

OEDIPUS:

But since God hates me . . .

CREON:

No, he will grant your wish.

OEDIPUS·

You promise?

CREON:

I can not speak beyond my knowledge.

OEDIPUS:

Then lead me in.

CREON:

Come now, and leave your children.

OEDIPUS:

No! Do not take them from me!

CREON:

Think no longer
That you are in command here, but rather think
How, when you were, you served your own destruc-
tion.

[Exeunt into the house all but the CHORUS;
the CHORAGOS chants directly to the audience:

CHORAGOS:

Men of Thebes: look upon Oedipus.

This is the king who solved the famous riddle
And towered up, most powerful of men.
No mortal eyes but looked on him with envy,
Yet in the end ruin swept over him.

Let every man in mankind's frailty
Consider his last day; and let none
Presume on his good fortune until he find
Life, at his death, a memory without pain.

◆§ Oedipus at Colonus

AN ENGLISH VERSION
BY ROBERT FITZGERALD

TO THE MEMORY OF MILMAN PARRY

"Nous vivons éternellement, non dans les écoles de pointilleurs de syllabes, mais dans le cercle des sages où l'on ne discute pas sur la mère d'Andromaque ou les fils de Niobé, mais où l'on s'entretient des origines profondes des choses divines et humaines."

PERSONS REPRESENTED:

OEDIPUS
ANTIGONE
A STRANGER
ISMENE
THESEUS
CREON
POLYNEICES
A MESSENGER
THE CHORUS

THE SCENE, *like the theater, is in the open air. In the background is the grove of the Furies at Colonus in Attica, about a mile northwest of Athens. A statue or stele of Colonus, a legendary horseman and hero, can be seen stage left. Stage right, a flat rock jutting out among the trees of the grove. Downstage, center, another ridge of rock.*

THE TIME: *early afternoon of a day about twenty years after the action of* Oedipus Rex.

◁§ SCENE I

[OEDIPUS, *old, blind, bearded and ragged, enters stage right, led by* ANTIGONE.

OEDIPUS:
My daughter—daughter of the blind old man—
Where have we come to now, Antigonê?

What lands are these, or holdings of what city?
Who will be kind to Oedipus this evening
And give alms to the wanderer?

Though he ask little and receive still less,
It is sufficient:
                    Suffering and time,
Vast time, have been instructors in contentment,
Which kingliness teaches too.
                              But now, child,
If you can see a resting place—perhaps
A roadside fountain, or some holy grove,
Tell me, and let me pause there and sit down;
So we may learn our whereabouts, and take
Our cue from what we hear, as strangers should.

ANTIGONE:

Father, poor tired Oedipus, the towers
That crown the city still seem far away;
As for this place, it is clearly a holy one,
Shady with vines and olive trees and laurel;—
A covert for the song and hush of nightingales
In their snug wings.
                     But rest on this rough stone.
It was a long road for an old man to travel.

OEDIPUS:

Help me sit down; take care of the blind man.

ANTIGONE:

After so long, you need not tell me, father.

OEDIPUS:

What can you say, now, as to where we are?

ANTIGONE:

This place I do not know; I know the city
Must be Athens

OEDIPUS:

As all the travellers said.

ANTIGONE:

Then shall I go and ask what place this is?

OEDIPUS:

Do, child, if there is any life near-by.

ANTIGONE:

Oh, but indeed there is; I need not leave you;
I see a man, now, not far away from us.

OEDIPUS:

Is he coming this way? Has he started toward us?
[*The* STRANGER *enters, left.*

ANTIGONE:

Here he is now.
                    Say what seems best to you,
Father; the man is here.

OEDIPUS:

Friend, my daughter's eyes serve for my own.
She tells me we are fortunate enough to meet you,
And no doubt you will inform us—

STRANGER:

                    Do not go on;
First move from where you sit; the place is holy;
It is forbidden to walk upon that ground.

OEDIPUS:

What ground is this? What god is honored here?

STRANGER:

> It is not to be touched, no one may live upon it;
> Most dreadful are its divinities, most feared,
> Daughters of darkness and mysterious earth.

OEDIPUS:

> Under what solemn name shall I invoke them?

STRANGER:

> The people here prefer to address them as Gentle
> All-seeing Ones; elsewhere there are other names.

OEDIPUS:

> Then may they be gentle to the suppliant.
> For I shall never leave this resting place.

STRANGER:

> What is the meaning of this?

OEDIPUS:

> It was ordained;
> I recognize it now.

STRANGER:

> Without authority
> From the city government I dare not move you;
> First I must show them what you are doing.

OEDIPUS:

> Friend, in the name of God, bear with me now!
> I turn to you for light; answer the wanderer.

STRANGER:

> Speak. You will have no discourtesy from me.

OEDIPUS:

> What is this region that we two have entered?

STRANGER:

As much as I can tell you, I will tell.
This country, all of it, is blessed ground;
The god Poseidon loves it; in it the firecarrier
Prometheus has his influence; in particular
That spot you rest on has been called this earth's
Doorsill of Brass, and buttress of great Athens.
All men of this land claim descent from him
Who is sculptured here: Colonus, master horseman,
And bear his name in common with their own.
That is this country, stranger: honored less
In histories than in the hearts of the people.

OEDIPUS:

Then people live here on their lands?

STRANGER:

                                        They do,
The clan of those descended from that hero.

OEDIPUS:

Ruled by a prince, or by the greater number?

STRANGER:

The land is governed from Athens, by the king.

OEDIPUS:

And who is he whose word has power here?

STRANGER:

Theseus, son of Aegeus, the king before him.

OEDIPUS:

Ah. Would someone then go to this king for me?

STRANGER:

To tell him what? Perhaps to urge his coming?

OEDIPUS:

To tell him a small favor will gain him much.

STRANGER:

What service can a blind man render him?

OEDIPUS:

All I shall say will be clear-sighted indeed.

STRANGER:

Friend, listen to me: I wish you no injury;
You seem well-born, though obviously unlucky;
Stay where you are, exactly where I found you,
And I'll inform the people of what you say—
Not in the town, but here—it rests with them
To decide if you should stay or must move on.

[*Exit* STRANGER, *left.*

OEDIPUS:

Child, has he gone?

ANTIGONE:

Yes, father. Now you may speak tranquilly,
For only I am with you.

OEDIPUS: [*Praying*
                    Ladies whose eyes
Are terrible: Spirits: upon your sacred ground
I have first bent my knees in this new land;
Therefore be mindful of me and of Apollo,
For when he gave me oracles of evil,
He also spoke of this:
                    A resting place,
After long years. in the last country, where
I should find home among the sacred Furies:
That I might round out there my bitter life.

Conferring benefit on those who received me,
A curse on those who have driven me away.

Portents, he said, would make me sure of this:
Earthquake, thunder, or God's smiling lightning;
But I am sure of it now, sure that you guided me
With feathery certainty upon this road,
And led me here into your hallowed wood.

How otherwise could I, in my wandering,
Have sat down first with you in all this land,
I who drink not, with you who love not wine?

How otherwise had I found this chair of stone?
Grant me then, goddesses, passage from life at last,
And consummation, as the unearthly voice foretold;
Unless indeed I seem not worth your grace:
Slave as I am to such unending pain
As no man had before.
                    O hear my prayer,
Sweet children of original Darkness! Hear me,
Athens, city named for great Athena,
Honored above all cities in the world!
Pity a man's poor carcase and his ghost,
For Oedipus is not the strength he was.

ANTIGONE:

Be still. Some old, old men are coming this way,
Looking for the place where you are seated.

OEDIPUS:

I shall be still. Take me clear of the path,
And hide me in the wood, so I may hear
What they are saying. If we know their temper
We shall be better able to act with prudence.
        [OEDIPUS *and* ANTIGONE *withdraw into the grove*

◄§ CHORAL DIALOGUE

[*The* CHORUS *enters from the left. Here,
and throughout the play, its lines may be
taken by various members as seems suit-
able.*]

CHORUS:

Look for him. Who could he be? Where
Is he? Where is the stranger
Impious, blasphemous, shameless!
Use your eyes, search him out!
Cover the ground and uncover him!
 Vagabond!
The old man must be a vagabond,
Not of our land, for he'd never
Otherwise dare to go in there,
In the inviolate thicket
Of those whom it's futile to fight,
Those whom we tremble to name.
When we pass we avert our eyes—
 Close our eyes!—
In silence, without conversation,
Shaping our prayers with our lips
But now, if the story is credible,
Some alien fool has profaned it;
Yet I have looked over all the grove and
 Still cannot see him;
Cannot say where he has hidden.
 [OEDIPUS *comes forward from the wood.*

OEDIPUS:

That stranger is I. As they say of the blind,
Sounds are the things I see.

CHORUS:

                    Ah!
His face is dreadful! His voice is dreadful!

OEDIPUS:

I beg you not to think me a criminal.

CHORUS:

Zeus defend us, who is this old man?

OEDIPUS:

One whose fate is not quite to be envied,
O my masters, and men of this land;
That must be evident: why, otherwise,
        Should I need this girl
To lead me, her frailty to put my weight on?

CHORUS:

Ah! His eyes are blind!
And were you brought into the world so?
Unhappy life—and so long!
Well, not if I can stop it,
Will you have this curse as well.—
        Stranger! you
Trespass there! But beyond there,
In the glade where the grass is still,
Where the honeyed libations drip
In the rill from the brimming spring,
You must not step! O stranger,
It is well to be careful about it!
        Most careful!
Stand aside and come down then!
There is too much space between us!
Say, wanderer, can you hear?
If you have a mind to tell us

Your business, or wish to converse with our council,
Come down from that place!
Only speak where it's proper to do so!

OEDIPUS:

Now, daughter, what is the way of wisdom?

ANTIGONE:

We must do just as they do here, father;
We should give in now, and listen to them.

OEDIPUS:

Stretch out your hand to me.

ANTIGONE

There, I am near you.

OEDIPUS:

Sirs, let there be no injustice done me,
Once I have trusted you, and left my refuge.
[Led by ANTIGONE, he starts downstage.

CHORUS:

Never, never, will anyone drive you away
From rest in this land, old man!

OEDIPUS:

Shall I come farther?

CHORUS:

Yes, farther.

OEDIPUS:

And now?

CHORUS:

You must guide him, girl;
You can see how far to come.

ANTIGONE:

Come with your blind step, father;
This way; come where I lead you.

CHORUS:

Stranger in a strange country,
Courage, afflicted man!
Whatever the state abhors
You, too, abhor; and honor
Whatever the state holds dear.

OEDIPUS:

Lead me on, then, child,
To where we may speak or listen respectfully;
Let us not fight necessity.

CHORUS:

Now! Go no farther than that platform there,
Formed of the natural rock.

OEDIPUS:

This?

CHORUS:

Far enough; you can hear us.

OEDIPUS:

Shall I sit down?

CHORUS:

Yes, sit there
To the left on the ridge of the rock.

ANTIGONE:

Father, this is where I can help you;
You must keep step with me; gently now.

OEDIPUS:

Ah, me!

ANTIGONE:

Lean your old body on my arm;
It is I, who love you; let yourself down.

OEDIPUS:

How bitter blindness is!

[*He is seated on the rock downstage, center.*

CHORUS:

Now that you are at rest, poor man,
Tell us, what is your name?
Who are you, wanderer?
What is the land of your ancestors?

OEDIPUS:

I am an exile, friends; but do not ask me . . .

CHORUS:

What is it you fear to say, old man?

OEDIPUS:

No, no, no! Do not go on
Questioning me! Do not ask my name!

CHORUS:

Why not?

OEDIPUS:

My star was unspeakable.

CHORUS:

Speak!

OEDIPUS:

My child, what can I say to them?

CHORUS:

Answer us, stranger; what is your race,
Who was your father?

OEDIPUS:

God help me, what will become of me, child?

ANTIGONE:

Tell them; there is no other way.

OEDIPUS:

Well, then, I will; I cannot hide it.

CHORUS:

Between you, you greatly delay. Speak up!

OEDIPUS:

Have you heard of Laius' family?

CHORUS:

Ah!

OEDIPUS:

Of the race of Labdacidae?

CHORUS:

Ah, Zeus!

OEDIPUS:

And ruined Oedipus?

CHORUS:

You are he!

OEDIPUS:

Do not take fright from what I say—

CHORUS:

Oh, dreadful!

OEDIPUS:

I am accursed.

CHORUS:

Oh, fearful!

OEDIPUS:

Antigonê, what will happen now?

CHORUS:

Away with you! Out with you! Leave our country!

OEDIPUS:

And what of the promises you made me?

CHORUS:

God will not punish the man
Who makes return for an injury:
Deceivers may be deceived:
They play a game that ends
In grief, and not in pleasure.
Leave this grove at once!
Our country is not for you!
Wind no further
Your clinging evil upon us!

ANTIGONE:

O men of reverent mind!
Since you will not suffer my father,
Old man though he is,

And though you know his story—
He never knew what he did—
Take pity still on my unhappiness,
And let me intercede with you for him.
Not with lost eyes, but looking in your eyes
As if I were a child of yours, I beg
Mercy for him, the beaten man! O hear me!
We are thrown upon your mercy as on God's;
    Be kinder than you seem!
By all you have and own that is dear to you:
Children, wives, possessions, gods, I pray you!
For you will never see in all the world
    A man whom God has led
    Escape his destiny!

◆§ SCENE II

CHORUS:

    Child of Oedipus, indeed we pity you,
    Just as we pity him for his misfortune;
    But we tremble to think of what the gods may do;
    We dare not speak more generously!

OEDIPUS:

    What use is reputation then? What good
    Comes of a noble name? A noble fiction!
    For Athens, so they say, excels in piety;
    Has power to save the wretched of other lands;
    Can give them refuge; is unique in this.
    Yet, when it comes to me, where is her refuge?
    You pluck me from these rocks and cast me out,
    All for fear of a name!
             Or do you dread
    My strength? my actions? I think not, for I

Suffered those deeds more than I acted them,
As I might show if it were fitting here
To tell my father's and my mother's story
For which you fear me, as I know too well.

And yet, how was I evil in myself?
I had been wronged, I retaliated; even had I
Known what I was doing, was that evil?
Then, knowing nothing, I went on. Went on.
But those who wronged me knew, and ruined me.

Therefore I beg of you before the gods,
For the same cause that made you move me—
In reverence of your gods—give me this shelter,
And thus accord those powers what is theirs.
Think: their eyes are fixed upon the just,
Fixed on the unjust, too; no impious man
Can twist away from them forever.
Now, in their presence, do not blot your city's
Luster by bending to unholy action;
As you would receive an honest petitioner,
Give me, too, sanctuary; though my face
Be dreadful in its look, yet honor me!

For I come here as one endowed with grace
By those who are over Nature; and I bring
Advantage to this race, as you may learn
More fully when some lord of yours is here.
Meanwhile be careful to be just.

CHORUS:

                              Old man,
This argument of yours compels our wonder.
It was not feebly worded. I am content
That higher authorities should judge this matter.

OEDIPUS:

And where is he who rules the land, strangers?

CHORUS:

In his father's city; but the messenger
Who sent us here has gone to fetch him also.

OEDIPUS:

Do you think a blind man will so interest him
As to bring him such a distance?

CHORUS:

I do, indeed, when he has heard your name.

OEDIPUS:

But who will tell him that?

CHORUS:

It is a long road, and the rumors of travellers
Have a way of wandering. He will have word of them;
Take heart—he will be here. Old man, your name
Has gone over all the earth; though he may be
At rest when the news comes, he will come quickly.

OEDIPUS:

Then may he come with luck for his own city,
As well as for me . . . The good befriend themselves.

ANTIGONE:

O Zeus! What shall I say? How interpret this?

OEDIPUS:

Antigonê, my dear child, what is it?

ANTIGONE:

                           A woman
Riding a Sicilian pony and coming toward us;
She is wearing a wide Thessalian sun-hat;
I don't know!

Is it or isn't it? Or am I dreaming?
I think so; yes!—No. I can't be sure. . . .

Ah, poor child,
It is no one else but she! And she is smiling
Now as she comes! It is my dear Ismenê!

OEDIPUS:

What did you say, child?

[ISMENE *enters, with one Attendant.*

ANTIGONE:

That I see your daughter!
My sister! Now you can tell her by her voice.

ISMENE:

O father and sister together! Dearest voices!
Now I have found you—how, I scarcely know—
I don't know how I shall see you through my tears!

OEDIPUS:

Child, have you come?

ISMENE:

Father, how old you seem!

OEDIPUS:

Child, are you here?

ISMENE:

And such a time I had!

OEDIPUS:

Touch me, little one.

ISMENE:

I shall hold you both!

OEDIPUS:

My children . . . and sisters.

ISMENE:

Oh, unhappy people!

OEDIPUS:

She and I?

ISMENE:

And I with you, unhappy.

OEDIPUS:

Why have you come, child?

ISMENE:

Thinking of you, father.

OEDIPUS:

You were lonely?

ISMENE:

Yes; and I bring news for you.
I came with the one person I could trust.

OEDIPUS:

Why, where are your brothers? Could they not do it?

ISMENE:

They are—where they are. It is a hard time for them

OEDIPUS:

Ah! They behave as if they were Egyptians,
Bred the Egyptian way! Down there, the men
Sit indoors all day long, weaving;
The women go out and attend to business.

Just so your brothers, who should have done this work
Sit by the fire like home-loving girls,
And you two, in their place, must bear my hardships.

One, since her childhood ended and her body
Gained its power, has wandered ever with me,
An old man's governess; often in the wild
Forest going without shoes, and hungry,
Beaten by many rains, tired by the sun;
Yet she rejected the sweet life of home
So that her father should have sustenance.

And you, my daughter, once before came out,
Unknown to Thebes, bringing me news of all
The oracle had said concerning me;
And you remained my faithful outpost there,
When I was driven from that land.
                                    But now,
What news, Ismenê, do you bring your father?
Why have you left your house to make this journey?
You came for no light reason, I know that;
It must be something serious for me.

ISMENE:

I will pass over the troubles I have had
Searching for your whereabouts, father.
They were hard enough to bear; and I will not
Go through it all again in telling of them.
In any case, it is your sons' troubles
That I have come to tell you.
First it was their desire, as it was Creon's,
That the throne should pass to him; that thus the city
Should be defiled no longer: such was their reasoning
When they considered our people's ancient curse
And how it enthralled your pitiful family.
But then some fury put it in their hearts—

O pitiful again!—to itch for power:
For seizure of prerogative and throne;
And it was the younger and the less mature
Who stripped his elder brother, Polyneicês,
Of place and kingship, and then banished him.

But now the people hear he has gone to Argos,
Into the valley land, has joined that nation,
And is enlisting friends among its warriors,
Telling them Argos shall honorably win
Thebes and her plain, or else eternal glory.
This is not a mere recital, father;
But terrible truth!
                    How long will it be, I wonder,
Before the gods take pity on your distress?

OEDIPUS:

You have some hope then that they are concerned
With my deliverance?

ISMENE:

                    I have, father.
The latest sentences of the oracle . . .

OEDIPUS:

How are they worded? What do they prophesy?

ISMENE:

That you shall be much solicited by our people
Before your death—and after—for their welfare.

OEDIPUS:

And what could anyone hope from such as I?

ISMENE:

The oracles declare their strength's in you—

OEDIPUS:

When I am worn to nothing, strength in me?

ISMENE:

For the gods who threw you down sustain you now.

OEDIPUS:

Slight favor, now I am old! My doom was early.

ISMENE:

The proof of it is that Creon is coming to you
For that same reason, and soon: not by and by.

OEDIPUS:

To do what, daughter? Tell me about this.

ISMENE:

To settle you near the land of Thebes, and so
Have you at hand; but you may not cross the border.

OEDIPUS:

What good am I to Thebes outside the country?

ISMENE:

It is merely that if your burial were unlucky,
That would be perilous for them.

OEDIPUS:

                                    Ah, then!
This does not need divine interpretation.

ISMENE:

Therefore they want to keep you somewhere near,
Just at the border, where you'll not be free.

OEDIPUS:

And will they compose my shade with Theban dust?

ISMENE:

Ah, father! No. Your father's blood forbids it.

OEDIPUS:

Then they shall never hold me in their power!

ISMENE:

If not, some day it will be bitter for them.

OEDIPUS:

How will that be, my child?

ISMENE:

                     When they shall stand
Where you are buried, and feel your anger there.

OEDIPUS:

This that you say—from whom did you hear it, child?

ISMENE:

The envoys told me when they returned from Delphi

OEDIPUS:

Then all this about me was spoken there?

ISMENE:

According to those men, just come to Thebes.

OEDIPUS:

Has either of my sons had word of this?

ISMENE:

They both have, and they understand it well.

OEDIPUS:

The scoundrels! So they knew all this, and yet
Would not give up the throne to have me back?

ISMENE:

It hurts me to hear it, but I can't deny it.

OEDIPUS:

Gods!
Never quench their fires of ambition!
Let the last word be mine upon this battle
They are about to join, with the spears lifting!
I'd see that he who holds the sceptre now
Would not have power long, nor would the other,
The banished one, return!
These were the two
Who saw me in disgrace and banishment
And never lifted a hand for me. They heard me
Howled from the country, heard the thing proclaimed!

And will they say I wanted exile then,
An appropriate clemency, granted by the state?
That is all false! The truth is that at first
My mind was a boiling caldron; nothing so sweet
As death, death by stoning, could have been given me;
Yet no one there would grant me that desire.
It was only later, when my madness cooled,
And I had begun to think my rage excessive,
My punishment too great for what I had done;
Then it was that the city—in its good time!—
Decided to be harsh, and drove me out.
They could have helped me then; they could have
Helped him who begot them! Would they do it?
For lack of a little word from that fine pair
Out I went, like a beggar, to wander forever!
Only by grace of these two girls, unaided,

Have I got food or shelter or devotion;
The others held their father of less worth
Than sitting on a throne and being king.

Well, they shall never win me in their fight!
Nor will they profit from the rule of Thebes.
I am sure of that; I have heard the prophecies
Brought by this girl; I think they fit those others
Spoken so long ago, and now fulfilled.
So let Creon be sent to find me: Creon,
Or any other of influence in the state.
If you men here consent—as do those powers
Holy and awful, the spirits of this place—
To give me refuge, then shall this city have
A great savior; and woe to my enemies!

CHORUS:

Oedipus: you are surely worth our pity:
You, and your children, too. And since you claim
Also to be a savior of our land,
I'd like to give you counsel for good luck.

OEDIPUS:

Dear friend! I'll do whatever you advise.

CHORUS:

Make expiation to these divinities
Whose ground you violated when you came.

OEDIPUS:

In what way shall I do so? Tell me, friends.

CHORUS:

First you must bring libations from the spring
That runs forever; and bring them with clean hands.

OEDIPUS:

And when I have that holy water, then?

CHORUS:

There are some bowls there, by a skillful potter;
Put chaplets round the brims, over the handles.

OEDIPUS:

Of myrtle sprigs, or woolen stuff? Of what?

CHORUS:

Take the fleeces cropped from a young lamb.

OEDIPUS:

Just so; then how must I perform the rite?

CHORUS:

Facing the quarter of the morning light,
Pour your libations out.

OEDIPUS:

Am I to pour them from the bowls you speak of?

CHORUS:

In three streams, yes; the last one, empty it.

OEDIPUS:

With what should it be filled? Tell me this, too.

CHORUS:

With water and honey; but with no wine added.

OEDIPUS:

And when the leaf-dark earth receives it?

CHORUS:

Lay three times nine young shoots of olive on it
With both your hands; meanwhile repeat this prayer:

OEDIPUS:

I am eager to hear this, for it has great power.

CHORUS:

That as we call them Eumenidês,
Which means the gentle of heart,
May they accept with gentleness
The suppliant and his wish.

So you, or he who prays for you, address them;

But do not speak aloud or raise a cry;
Then come away, and do not turn again.
If you will do all this, I shall take heart
And stand up for you; otherwise, O stranger,
I should be seriously afraid for you.

OEDIPUS:

Children, you hear the words of these good people?

ANTIGONE:

Yes; now tell us what we ought to do.

OEDIPUS:

It need not be performed by me; I'm far
From having strength or sight for it—I have neither.
Let one of you go and carry out the ritual.
One soul, I think, often can make atonement
For many others, if it be devoted.
Now do it quickly.—Yet do not leave me alone!
I could not move without the help of someone.

ISMENE:

I'll go and do it. But where am I to go?
Where shall I find the holy place, I wonder?

CHORUS:

On the far side of the wood, girl. If you need it,
You may get help from the attendant there.

ISMENE:

I am going now. Antigonê, you will stay
And care for father. If it were difficult,
I should not think it so, since it is for him.
          [ISMENE *goes out, right. The* CHORUS *draws
          nearer to* OEDIPUS.

◄§ CHORAL DIALOGUE

CHORUS:

What evil things have slept since long ago
It is not sweet to waken;
And yet I long to be told—

OEDIPUS:

                              What?

CHORUS:

Of that heartbreak for which there was no help,
The pain you have had to suffer.

OEDIPUS:

For kindness' sake, do not open
My old wound, and my shame.

CHORUS:

It is told everywhere, and never dies;
I only want to hear it truly told.

OEDIPUS:

Ah! Ah!

CHORUS:

Consent I beg you;
Give me my wish, and I shall give you yours.

OEDIPUS:

I had to face a thing most terrible,
Not willed by me, I swear;
I would have abhorred it all.

CHORUS:

So?

OEDIPUS:

Though I did not know, Thebes married me to evil;
Fate and I were joined there.

CHORUS:

Then it was indeed your mother
With whom the thing was done?

OEDIPUS:

Ah! It is worse than death to have to hear it!
Strangers! Yes: and these two girls of mine . . .

CHORUS:

You say—?

OEDIPUS:

These luckless two
Were given birth by her who gave birth to me.

CHORUS:

These then are daughters; they are also—

OEDIPUS:

Sisters: yes, their father's sisters . . .

CHORUS:

Ah, pity!

OEDIPUS:

Pity, indeed. What throngs
Of pities come into my mind!

CHORUS:

You suffered—

OEDIPUS:

Yes, unspeakably.

CHORUS:

You sinned—

OEDIPUS:

No, I did not sin!

CHORUS:

How not?

OEDIPUS:

I thought
Of her as my reward. Ah, would that I had never won it!
Would that I had never served the State that day!

CHORUS:

Unhappy man—and you also killed—

OEDIPUS:

What is it now? What are you after?

CHORUS:

Killed your father!

OEDIPUS:

God in heaven!
You strike again where I am hurt.

CHORUS:

You killed him.

OEDIPUS:

Killed him. Yet there is—

CHORUS:

What more?

OEDIPUS:

A just extenuation.
This:
I did not know him; and he wished to murder me.
Before the law—before God—I am innocent!
                    [*The* CHORUS *turns at the approach of* THESEUS

∙§ SCENE III

CHORUS:

The king is coming! Aegeus' eldest son,
Theseus: news of you has brought him here.
                    [THESEUS *enters with soldiers, left.*

THESEUS:

In the old time I often heard men tell
Of the bloody extinction of your eyes.
Even if on my way I were not informed,
I'd recognize you, son of Laius.
The garments and the tortured face
Make plain your identity. I am sorry for you.
And I should like to know what favor here
You hope for from the city and from me:
Both you and your unfortunate companion.
Tell me. It would be something dire indeed
To make me leave you comfortless; for I
Too was an exile. I grew up abroad,
And in strange lands I fought as few men have
With danger and with death.
Therefore no wanderer shall come, as you do,
And be denied my audience or aid.
I know I am only a man; I have no more
To hope for in the end than you have.

OEDIPUS:

Theseus, in those few words your nobility
Is plain to me. I need not speak at length;
You have named me and my father accurately,
Spoken with knowledge of my land and exile.
There is, then, nothing left for me to tell
But my desire; and then the tale is ended.

THESEUS:

Tell me your wish, then; let me hear it now.

OEDIPUS:

I come to give you something, and the gift
Is my own beaten self: no feast for the eyes;
Yet in me is a more lasting grace than beauty.

THESEUS:

What grace is this you say you bring to us?

OEDIPUS:

In time you'll learn, but not immediately.

THESEUS:

How long, then, must we wait to be enlightened?

OEDIPUS:

Until I am dead, and you have buried me.

THESEUS:

Your wish is burial? What of your life meanwhile?
Have you forgotten that?—or do you care?

OEDIPUS:

It is all implicated in my burial.

THESEUS:

But this is a brief favor you ask of me.

OEDIPUS:

See to it, nevertheless! It is not simple.

THESEUS:

You mean I shall have trouble with your sons?

OEDIPUS:

Those people want to take me back there now.

THESEUS:

Will you not go? Is exile admirable?

OEDIPUS:

No. When I wished to go, they would not have
it.

THESEUS:

What childishness! You are surely in no position—

OEDIPUS:

When you know me, admonish me; not now!

THESEUS:

Instruct me, then. I must not speak in ignorance.

OEDIPUS:

Theseus, I have been wounded more than once.

THESEUS:

Is it your family's curse that you refer to?

OEDIPUS:

Not merely that; all Hellas talks of that.

THESEUS:

Then what is the wound that is so pitiless?

OEDIPUS:

Think how it is with me. I was expelled
From my own land by my own sons; and now,
As a parricide, my return is not allowed.

THESEUS:

How can they summon you, if this is so?

OEDIPUS:

The sacred oracle compels them to.

THESEUS:

They fear some punishment from his forebodings?

OEDIPUS:

They fear they will be struck down in this land!

THESEUS:

And how could war arise between these nations?

OEDIPUS:

Most gentle son of Aegeus! The immortal
Gods alone have neither age nor death!
All other things almighty Time disquiets.
Earth wastes away; the body wastes away;
Faith dies; distrust is born.
And imperceptibly the spirit changes
Between a man and his friend, or between two cities.
For some men soon, for others in later time,
Their pleasure sickens; or love comes again.
And so with you and Thebes: the sweet season
Holds between you now; but time goes on,
Unmeasured Time, fathering numberless
Nights, unnumbered days: and on one day
They'll break apart with spears this harmony—
All for a trivial word.
And then my sleeping and long-hidden corpse,
Cold in the earth, will drink hot blood of theirs,
If Zeus endures; if his son's word is true.

However: there's no felicity in speaking
Of hidden things. Let me come back to this:
Be careful that you keep your word to me;
For if you do you'll never say of Oedipus
That he was given refuge uselessly—
Or if you say it, then the gods have lied.

CHORUS:

My lord: before you came this man gave promise
Of having power to make his words come true.

THESEUS:

Who would reject his friendship? Is he not
One who would have, in any case, an ally's

Right to our hospitality?
Moreover he has asked grace of our deities,
And offers no small favor in return.
As I value this favor, I shall not refuse
This man's desire; I declare him a citizen.

And if it should please our friend to remain here,
I direct you to take care of him;
Or else he may come with me.
                        Whatever you choose,
Oedipus, we shall be happy to accord.
You know your own needs best; I accede to them.

OEDIPUS:

May God bless men like these!

THESEUS:

What do you say then? Shall it be my house?

OEDIPUS:

If it were right for me. But the place is here . . .

THESEUS:

And what will you do here?—Not that I oppose you.

OEDIPUS:

Here I shall prevail over those who banished me.

THESEUS:

Your presence, as you say, is a great blessing.

OEDIPUS:

If you are firm in doing what you promise.

THESEUS:

You can be sure of me; I'll not betray you.

OEDIPUS:

I'll not ask pledges, as I would of scoundrels.

THESEUS:

You'd get no more assurance than by my word.

OEDIPUS:

I wonder how you will behave?

THESEUS:

You fear?

OEDIPUS:

That men will come—

THESEUS:

These men will attend to them

OEDIPUS:

Look: when you leave me—

THESEUS:

I know what to do!

OEDIPUS:

I am oppressed by fear!

THESEUS:

I feel no fear.

OEDIPUS:

You do not know the menace!

THESEUS:

I do know
No man is going to take you against my will.
Angry men are liberal with threats

And bluster generally. When the mind
Is master of itself, threats are no matter.
These people may have dared to talk quite fiercely
Of taking you; perhaps, as I rather think,
They'll find a sea of troubles in the way.
Therefore I should advise you to take heart.
Even aside from me and my intentions,
Did not Apollo send and guide you here?
However it may be, I can assure you,
While I'm away, my name will be your shield.

> [*Exit* THESEUS *and soldiers. The* CHORUS
> *turns to the audience.*

⋑ CHORAL POEM

CHORUS:

The land of running horses, fair
Colonus takes a guest;
He shall not seek another home,
For this, in all the earth and air,
Is most secure and loveliest.

In the god's untrodden vale
Where leaves and berries throng,
And wine-dark ivy climbs the bough,
The sweet, sojourning nightingale
Murmurs all night long.

No sun nor wind may enter there
Nor the winter's rain;
But ever through the shadow goes
Dionysus reveler,
Immortal maenads in his train.

Here with drops of heaven's dews
At daybreak all the year,

The clusters of narcissus bloom,
Time-hallowed garlands for the brows
Of those great ladies whom we fear.

The crocus like a little sun
Blooms with its yellow ray;
The river's fountains are awake,
And his nomadic streams that run
Unthinned forever, and never stay;

But like perpetual lovers move
On the maternal land.
And here the choiring Muses come,
And the divinity of love
With gold reins in her hand.
            [*The* CHORUS *may now shift its grouping*
               or otherwise indicate a change of theme.

CHORUS:

And our land has a thing unknown
On Asia's sounding coast
Or in the sea-surrounded west
Where Pelop's kin hold sway:
The olive, fertile and self-sown,
The terror of our enemies
That no hand tames or tears away—
The blessed tree that never dies!—
But it will mock the swordsman in his rage.

Ah, how it flourishes in every field,
Most beautifully here!
The grey-leafed tree, the children's nourisher!
No young man nor one partnered by his age
Knows how to root it out nor make
Barren its yield;
For Zeus Protector of the Shoot has sage
Eyes that forever are awake,
And Pallas watches with her sea-grey eyes.

Last and grandest praise I sing
To Athens, nurse of men,
For her great pride and for the splendor
Destiny has conferred on her.
Land from which fine horses spring!
Land where foals are beautiful!
Land of the sea and the sea-farer,
Enthroned on her pure littoral
By Cronus' briny son in ancient time.

That lord, Poseidon, must I praise again,
Who found our horsemen fit
For first bestowal of the curb and bit,
To discipline the stallion in his prime;
And strokes to which our oarsmen sing,
Well-fitted, oak and men,
Whose long sea-oars in wondrous rhyme
Flash from the salt foam, following
The track of winds on waters virginal.

> [At the conclusion of this, ANTIGONE is
> standing stage right, looking off-stage at-
> tentively.

⊷§ SCENE IV

ANTIGONE:

Land so well spoken of and praised so much!
Now is the time to show those words are true.

OEDIPUS:

What now, my child?

ANTIGONE: [Returning to him

A man is coming toward us,
And it is Creon—not alone, though, father.

OEDIPUS:

Most kindly friends! I hope you may give proof,
And soon, of your ability to protect me!

CHORUS:

No fear; it will be proved. I may be old
But the nation's strength has not grown old.
                    [*Enter* CREON, *right, with guards.*

CREON:

Gentlemen, and citizens of this land:
I can see from your eyes that my arrival
Has been a cause of sudden fear to you;
Do not be fearful. And say nothing hostile!
I have not come for any hostile action,
For I am old, and know this city has
Power, if any city in Hellas has.

But for this man here: I, despite my age,
Am sent to bring him to the land of Thebes.
Not one man's mission, this, but it was ordered
By the whole Theban people. I am their emissary
Because it fell to me as a relative
To mourn his troubles more than anyone.

So, now, poor Oedipus, come home.
You know the word I bring. Your countrymen
Are right in summoning you—I most of all,
For most of all, unless I am worst of men,
I grieve for your unhappiness, old man.
I see you ravaged as you are, a stranger
Everywhere, never at rest,
With only a girl to serve you in your need.—
I never thought she'd fall to such indignity,
Poor child! And yet she has;
Forever tending you, leading a beggar's

Life with you; a grown-up girl who knows
Nothing of marriage; whoever comes can take her.

Is this not a disgrace? I weep to see it!
Disgrace for you, for me, for all our people!
We cannot hide what is so palpable,
But you, if you will listen to me, Oedipus—
And in the name of your father's gods, listen!—
Bury the whole thing now; agree with me
To go back to your city and your home!

Take friendly leave of Athens, as she merits;
But you should have more reverence for Thebes,
Since long ago she was your kindly nurse.

OEDIPUS:

You brazen rascal! Playing your rascal's tricks
In righteous speeches, as you always would!
Why do you try it? How can you think to take me
Into that snare I should so hate if taken?

That time when I was sick with my own life's
Evil: when I would gladly have left the earth—
You had no mind to give me what I wanted!
But when at long last I had had my fill
Of rage and grief, and in my quiet house
Began to find some comfort: that was the time
You chose to rout me out.
How precious was this kinship then?
It is the same thing now: you see this city
And all its people being kind to me,
So you would draw me away—
A cruel thing, for all your soothing words.

Why is it your pleasure is to be amiable
To those who do not want your amiability?

Suppose that when you begged for something des-
  perately
A man should neither grant it you nor give
Sympathy even; but later when you were glutted
With all your heart's desire, should give it then,
When charity was no charity at all?
Would you not think the kindness somewhat hollow?
That is the sort of kindness you offer me:
Generous in words, but in reality evil.
Now I will tell these men, and prove you evil.
You come to take me, but not to take me home;
Rather to settle me outside the city
So that the city may escape my curse,
Escape from punishment by Athens.
                              Yes;
But you'll not have it. What you'll have is this:
My vengeance active in that land forever;
And what my sons will have of my old kingdom
Is just so much room as they need to die in!

Now who knows better the destiny of Thebes?
I do, for I have had the best informants:
Apollo, and Zeus himself who is his father.
And yet you come here with your fraudulent speech
All whetted up! The more you talk, the more
Harm, not good, you'll get by it!—
However, I know you'll never believe that.—

Only leave us! Let us live here in peace!
Is this misfortune if it brings contentment?

CREON:

Which of us do you consider is more injured
By talk like this? You hurt only yourself.

OEDIPUS:

I am perfectly content, so long as you
Can neither wheedle me nor fool these others.

CREON:

Unhappy man! Shall it be plain that time
Brings you no wisdom? that you shame your age?

OEDIPUS:

An agile wit! I know no honest man
Able to speak so well under all conditions!

CREON:

To speak much is one thing; to speak to the point
another!

OEDIPUS:

As if you spoke so little but so fittingly!

CREON:

No, not fittingly for a mind like yours!

OEDIPUS:

Leave me! I speak for these men, too!
Spare me your wardship, here where I must live!

CREON:

I call on these—not you!—as witnesses
Of what rejoinder you have made to friends.—
If I ever take you—

OEDIPUS:

                        With these men opposing,
Who is going to take me by violence?

CREON:

You'll suffer without need of that, I promise you!

OEDIPUS:

What are you up to? What is behind that brag?

CREON:

Your daughters: one of them I have just now
Had seized and carried off; now I'll take this one!

OEDIPUS:

Ah!

CREON:

Soon you shall have more reason to groan about it!

OEDIPUS:

You have my child?

CREON:

              And this one in a moment!

OEDIPUS:

Ah, friends! What will you do? Will you betray me?
Expel this man who has profaned your country!

CHORUS:

Go, and go quickly, stranger! You have no right
To do what you are doing, or what you have done!

CREON: [*To* GUARDS:

You there: it would be well to take her now,
Whether she wants to go with you or not.
           [*Two* GUARDS *approach* ANTIGONE.

ANTIGONE:

Oh, God, where shall I run? What help is there
From gods or men?

CHORUS:

             What are you doing, stranger?

CREON:

I will not touch this man; but she is mine.

OEDIPUS:
O masters of this land!

CHORUS:
This is unjust!

CREON:
No, just!

CHORUS:
Why so?

CREON:
I take what belongs to me!

OEDIPUS:
O Athens!

CHORUS:
What are you doing, strangers? Will you
Let her go? Must we have a test of strength?

CREON:
Keep off!

CHORUS:
I will not; you are chargeable!

CREON:
Your city will have war if you hurt me!

OEDIPUS:
Did I not proclaim this?

CHORUS: [To GUARDS:
                                      Take your hands
  Off the child at once!

CREON:
                      What you cannot enforce,
  Do not command!

CHORUS:
  Release the child, I say!

CREON:
                        And I say—March!
            [The GUARDS pull ANTIGONE toward the right.

CHORUS:
  Help! Here, men of Colonus! Help! Help!
  The city, my city, is violated!
  Help, ho!

ANTIGONE:
  They drag me away. How wretched! O friends, friends!

OEDIPUS: [Groping
  Where are you, child?

ANTIGONE:
                     They have overpowered me!

OEDIPUS:
  Give me your hands, little one!

ANTIGONE:
                  I cannot do it!

CREON: [To GUARDS:

Will you get on with her?

                        [They go out, right.

OEDIPUS:

                    God help me now!

CREON:

With these two sticks at any rate you'll never
Guide yourself again! But since you wish
To conquer your own people—by whose command,
Though I am royal, I have performed this act—
Go on and conquer! Later, I think, you'll learn
That now as before you have done yourself no good
By gratifying your temper against your friends!
Anger has always been your greatest sin!

CHORUS: [Approaching CREON

Control yourself, stranger!

CREON:

Don't touch me, I say!

CHORUS:

I'll not release you! Those two girls were stolen!

CREON:

By God, I'll have more booty in a moment
To bring my city! I'll not stop with them!

CHORUS:

Now what are you about?

CREON:

                    I'll take him. too!

CHORUS:

A terrible thing to say!

CREON:

It will be done!

CHORUS:

Not if the ruler of our land can help it!

OEDIPUS:

Voice of shamelessness! Will you touch me?

CREON:

Silence, I say!

OEDIPUS:

No! May the powers here
Not make me silent until I say this curse:
You scoundrel, who have cruelly taken her
Who served my naked eyepits as their eyes!
On you and yours forever may the sun god,
Watcher of all the world, confer such days
As I have had, and such an age as mine!

CREON:

Do you see this, men of the Land of Athens?

OEDIPUS:

They see both me and you; and they see also
That when I am hurt I have only words to avenge it!

CREON:

I'll not stand for it longer! Alone as I am,
And slow with age, I'll try my strength to take him!
                    [CREON *goes slowly toward* OEDIPUS.

OEDIPUS:

Ah!

CHORUS:

You are a bold man, friend,
If you think you can do this!

CREON:

I do think so!

CHORUS:

If you could, our city would be finished!

CREON:

In a just cause the weak will beat the strong!

OEDIPUS:

You hear his talk?

CHORUS:

By Zeus, he shall not do it!

CREON:

Zeus may determine that, but you will not.

CHORUS:

Is this not criminal!

CREON: [*Laying hold of* OEDIPUS

If so, you'll bear it!

CHORUS:

Ho, everyone! Captains, ho!
Come on the run!
They are well on their way by now!
[THESEUS *enters, left, with armed men.*

THESEUS:

Why do you shout? What is the matter here?
Of what are you afraid?
You have interrupted me as I was sacrificing
To the great sea god, the patron of Colonus.
Tell me, let me know everything.
I do not care to make such haste for nothing.

OEDIPUS:

O dearest friend—I recognize your voice—
A fearful thing has just been done to me!

THESEUS:

What is it? Who is the man who did it? Tell me.

OEDIPUS:

This Creon has had my daughters bound and stolen.

THESEUS:

What's this you say?

OEDIPUS:

Yes; now you know my loss.

THESEUS: [*To his men:*

One of you go on the double
To the altar place and rouse the people there;
Make them leave the sacrifice at once
And run full speed, both foot and cavalry
As hard as they can gallop, for the place
Where the two highways come together
The girls must not be taken past that point,
Or I shall be a laughing-stock to this fellow,
As if I were a man to be handled roughly!
Go on, do as I tell you! Quick!

[*Exit* SOLDIER, *left.*

This man—
If I should act in anger, as he deserves,
I would not let him leave my hands unbloodied;
But he shall be subject to the sort of laws
He has himself imported here.—

[*To* CREON:

You: you shall never leave this land of Attica
Until you produce those girls here in my presence;
For your behavior is an affront to me,
A shame to your own people and your nation.

You come to a city-state that practices justice,
A state that rules by law, and by law only;
And yet you cast aside her authority,
Take what you please, and worse, by violence,
As if you thought there were no men among us,
Or only slaves; and as if I were nobody.

I doubt that Thebes is responsible for you:
She has no propensity for breeding rascals.
And Thebes would not applaud you if she knew
You tried to trick me and to rob the gods
By dragging helpless people from their sanctuary!

Were I a visitor in your country—
No matter how immaculate my claims—
Without consent from him who ruled the land,
Whoever he might be, I should take nothing.
I think I have some notion of the conduct
Proper to one who visits a friendly city.
You bring disgrace upon an honorable
Land—your own land, too; a long life
Seems to have left you witless as you are old.

I said it once and say it now again:
Someone had better bring those girls here quickly,
Unless you wish to prolong your stay with us

Under close guard, and not much liking it.
This is not just a speech; I mean it, friend.

CHORUS:

Now do you see where you stand? Thebes is just,
But you are adjudged to have acted wickedly.

CREON:

It was not that I thought this state unmanly,
Son of Aegeus; nor ill-governed, either;
Rather I did this thing in the opinion
That no one here would love my citizens
So tenderly as to keep them against my will.
And surely, I thought, no one would give welcome
To an unholy man, a parricide,
A man with whom his mother had been found!
Such at least was my estimate of the wisdom
Native to the Areopagus; I thought
Athens was not a home for such exiles.
In that belief I considered him my prize.
Yet I should not have touched him, had he not
Called down curses on my race and me;
That was an injury that deserved reprisal.
There is no old age for a man's anger,
Only death; the dead cannot be hurt.

You will do as you wish in this affair,
For even though my case is right and just,
I am weak, without support. Nevertheless,
Old as I am, I'll try to hold you answerable.

OEDIPUS:

O arrogance unashamed! Whose age do you
Think you are insulting, mine or yours?
The bloody deaths, the incest, the calamities
You speak so glibly of: I suffered them,
By fate, against my will! It was God's pleasure,

And perhaps our race had angered him long ago.
In me myself you could not find such evil
As would have made me sin against my own.
And tell me this: if there were prophecies
Repeated by the oracles of the gods,
That Father's death should come through his own son,
How could you justly blame it upon me?
On me, who was yet unborn, yet unconceived,
Not yet existent for my father and mother?
If then I came into the world—as I did come—
In wretchedness, and met my father in fight,
And knocked him down, not knowing that I killed
    him
Nor whom I killed—again, how could you find
Guilt in that unmeditated act?
As for my mother—damn you, you have no shame,
Though you are her own brother, in forcing me
To speak of that unspeakable marriage;
But I shall speak, I'll not be silent now
After you let your foul talk go so far!
Yes, she gave me birth—incredible fate!—
But neither of us knew the truth; and she
Bore my children also—and then her shame.
But one thing I do know: you are content
To slander her as well as me for that;
While I would not have married her willingly
Nor willingly would I ever speak of it.

No: I shall not be judged an evil man,
Neither in that marriage nor in that death
Which you forever charge me with so bitterly.—
Just answer me one thing:
If someone tried to kill you here and now,
You righteous gentleman, what would you do,
Inquire first if the stranger was your father?
Or would you not first try to defend yourself?

I think that since you like to be alive
You'd treat him as the threat required; not
Look around for assurance that you were right.
Well, that was the sort of danger I was in,
Forced into it by the gods. My father's soul,
Were it on earth, I know would bear me out.

You, however, being a knave—and since you
Think it fair to say anything you choose,
And speak of what should not be spoken of—
Accuse me of all this before these people.
You also think it clever to flatter Theseus,
And Athens—her exemplary government;
But in your flattery you have forgotten this:
If any country comprehends the honors
Due to the gods, this country knows them best;
Yet you could steal me from Athens in my age
And in my time of prayer; indeed, you seized me,
And you have seized and carried off my daughters.

Now for that profanation I make my prayer,
Calling on the divinities of the grove
That they shall give me aid and fight for me;
So you may know what men defend this town.

CHORUS:

My lord, our friend is worthy; he has had
Disastrous fortune; yet he deserves our comfort.

THESEUS:

Enough of speeches. While the perpetrators
Flee, we who were injured loiter here.

CREON:

What will you have me do?—since I am worthless.

THESEUS:

You lead us on the way. You can be my escort.
If you are holding the children in this neighborhood

You yourself will uncover them to me.
If your retainers have taken them in flight,
The chase is not ours; others are after them.
And they will never have cause to thank their gods
For getting free out of this country.
All right. Move on. And remember that the captor
Is now the captive; the hunter is in the snare.
What was won by stealth will not be kept.

In this you will have no others to assist you;
And I know well you had them, for you'd never
Dare to go so far in your insolence
Were you without sufficient accomplices.
You must have had a reason for your confidence,
And I must reckon with it. The whole city
Must not seem overpowered by one man.
Do you understand at all? Or do you think
That what I say is still without importance?

CREON:

To what you say I make no objection here.
At home we, too, shall determine what to do.

THESEUS:

If you must threaten, do so on the way.
Oedipus, you stay here, and rest assured
That unless I perish first I'll not draw breath
Until I put your children in your hands.

OEDIPUS:

Bless you for your noble heart, Theseus!
And you are blessed in what you do for us!

[*Two* SOLDIERS *take* CREON *by the arms and
march him out, right, followed by* THESEUS
and the rest of his men. The CHORUS *follows a short way and stands gazing after
them.*

❧ CHORAL POEM

CHORUS:

Ah, God, to be where the pillagers make stand!
To hear the shout and brazen sound of war!
Or maybe on Apollo's sacred strand,
Or by that torchlit Eleusinian shore

Where pilgrims come, whose lips the golden key
Of sweet-voiced ministers has rendered still,
To cherish there with grave Persephonê
Consummate rest from death and mortal ill;

For even to those shades the warrior king
Will press the fighting on—until he take
The virgin sisters from the foemen's ring,
Within his country, for his country's sake!

It may be they will get beyond the plain
And reach the snowy mountain's western side,
If their light chariots have the racing rein,
If they have ponies, and if they can ride;

Yet they'll be taken: for the god they fear
Fights for our land, and Theseus sends forth
His headlong cavalry with all its gear
Flashing like mountain lightning to the north.

These are the riders of Athens, conquered never;
They honor her whose glory all men know,
And honor the sea god, who is dear forever
To Rhea Mother, who bore him long ago.
        [*A shift of grouping, and the following stan-
        zas taken each by a separate voice.*

CHORUS:

Swords out—or has the work of swords begun?
My mind leans to a whisper:
Within the hour they must surrender
The woeful children of the blinded one:
This day is shaped by Zeus Artificer.
I can call up the bright sword play,
But wish the wind would lift me like a dove
Under the tall cloud cover
To look with my own eyes on this affray.

Zeus, lord of all, and eye of heaven on all,
Let our Home Troop's hard riding
Cut them off, and a charge from hiding
Carry the combat in one shock and fall.
Stand, helmeted Athena, at our side.
Apollo, Artemis, come down,
Hunter and huntress of the flickering deer—
Pace with each cavalier
For honor of our land and Athens town.

> [*There is a long pause, and then the*
> CHORUS *turns to* OEDIPUS *in joy.*

•§ SCENE V

CHORUS:

O wanderer! You will not say I lied;
I who kept lookout for you!
I see them now—the two girls—here they come
With our armed men around them!

OEDIPUS:

What did you say? Ah, where?
> [THESEUS *comes in leading by the hand*
> ANTIGONE *and* ISMENE, *followed by* SOL-
> DIERS.

ANTIGONE:

                    O father, father!
I wish some god would give you eyes to see
The noble prince who brings us back to you!

OEDIPUS:

Ah, child! You are really here?

ANTIGONE:

                    Yes, for the might
Of Theseus and his kind followers saved us.

OEDIPUS:

Come to your father, child, and let me touch you
Whom I had thought never to touch again!

ANTIGONE:

It shall be as you ask; I wish it as much as you.

OEDIPUS:

Where are you?

ANTIGONE:

                        We are coming to you together.

OEDIPUS:

  My sweet children!

ANTIGONE:

                        To our father, sweet indeed.

OEDIPUS:

  My staff and my support!

ANTIGONE:

                        And partners in sorrow

OEDIPUS:

I have what is dearest to me in the world.
To die, now, would not be so terrible,
Since you are near me.
                Press close to me, child,
Be rooted in your father's arms; rest now
From the cruel separation, the going and coming;
And tell me the story as briefly as you can:
A little talk is enough for girls so tired.

ANTIGONE:

Theseus saved us: he is the one to tell you;
And he can put it briefly and make it clear.

OEDIPUS:

Dear friend: don't be offended if I continue
To talk to these two children overlong;
I had scarce thought they would be seen again!
Be sure I understand that you alone
Made this joy possible for me.
You are the one that saved them, no one else.

And may the gods give you such destiny
As I desire for you: and for your country.
For I have found you truly reverent,
Decent, and straight in speech: you only
Of all mankind.
I know it, and I thank you with these words.
All that I have I owe to your courtesy;—
Now give me your right hand, my lord,
And if it be permitted, let me kiss you.

What am I saying? How can a wretch like me
Desire to touch a man who has no stain
Of evil in him? No, no; I will not do it;
And neither shall you touch me. The only ones
Fit to be fellow-sufferers of mine
Are those with such experience as I have.
Receive my salutation where you are.
And for the rest, be kindly to me still
As you have been up to now.

THESEUS:

That you should talk a long time to your children
In joy at seeing them—why, that's no wonder!
Or that you should address them before me—
There's no offense in that. It is not in words
That I should wish my life to be distinguished,
But rather in things done.
Have I not shown that? I was not a liar
In what I swore I'd do for you, old man.
I am here; and I have brought them back
Alive and safe, for all they were threatened with.
As to how I found them, how I took them, why
Brag of it? You will surely learn from them.

However, there is a matter that just now
Came to my attention on my way here—

A trivial thing to speak of, and yet puzzling;
I want your opinion on it.
It is best for a man not to neglect such things.

OEDIPUS:

What is it, son of Aegeus? Tell me,
So I may know on what you desire counsel.

THESEUS:

They say a man has come here claiming to be
A relative of yours, though not of Thebes;
For some reason he has thrown himself in prayer
Before Poseidon's altar, where I was making
Sacrifice before I came.

OEDIPUS:

What is his country? What is he praying for?

THESEUS:

All I know is this: he asks, they tell me,
A brief interview with you, and nothing more.

OEDIPUS:

Upon what subject?
If he is in prayer, it cannot be a trifle.

THESEUS:

They say he only asks to speak to you
And then to depart safely by the same road.

OEDIPUS:

Who could it be who would come here to pray?

THESEUS:

Think: have you any relative in Argos
Who might desire this favor of you?

OEDIPUS:

Dear friend!
Say no more!

THESEUS:

What has alarmed you?

OEDIPUS:
No more!

THESEUS:

But: what is the matter? Tell me.

OEDIPUS:
When I heard "Argos" I knew the petitioner.

THESEUS:
And who is he whom I must hold at fault?

OEDIPUS:
A son of mine, my lord, and a hated one.
Nothing could be more painful than to listen to him.

THESEUS:
But why? Is it not possible to listen
Without doing anything you need not do?
Why should it distress you so to hear him?

OEDIPUS:
My lord, even his voice is hateful to me.
Don't overrule me; don't make me yield in this!

THESEUS:
But now consider if you are not obliged
To do so by his supplication here:
Perhaps you have a duty to the god.

ANTIGONE:

Father: listen to me, even if I am young.
Allow this man to satisfy his conscience
And give the gods whatever he thinks their due.
And let our brother come here, for my sake.
Don't be afraid: he will not throw you off
In your resolve, nor speak offensively.
What is the harm in hearing what he says?
If he has ill intentions, he'll betray them.
You sired him; even though he wronged you, father,
And wronged you impiously, still you can not
Rightfully wrong him in return!
Do let him come!
                    Other men have bad sons,
And other men are swift to anger: yet
They will accept advice, they will be swayed
By their friends' pleading, even against their nature.
Reflect, not on the present, but on the past;
Think of your mother's and your father's fate
And what you suffered through them! If you do,
I think you'll see how terrible an end
Terrible wrath may have.
You have, I think, a permanent reminder
In your lost, irrecoverable eyes.
Ah, yield to us! If our request is just,
We need not, surely, be importunate;
And you, to whom I have not yet been hard,
Should not be obdurate with me!

OEDIPUS:

Child, your talk wins you a pleasure
That will be a pain for me. If you have set
Your heart on it, so be it.

Only, Theseus: if he is to come here,
Let no one have power over my life!

THESEUS:

That is the sort of thing I need hear only
Once, not twice, old man. I do not boast,
But you should know your life is safe while mine is.
[THESEUS *goes out, left, with his* SOLDIERS,
leaving two on guard. The CHORUS *turns
to address the audience.*

◄§ CHORAL POEM

CHORUS:

Though he has watched a decent age pass by,
A man will sometimes still desire the world.
I swear I see no wisdom in that man.
The endless hours pile up a drift of pain
More unrelieved each day; and as for pleasure,
When he is sunken in excessive age,
You will not see his pleasure anywhere.
The last attendant is the same for all,
Old men and young alike, as in its season
Man's heritage of underworld appears:
There being then no epithalamion,
No music and no dance. Death is the finish.

Not to be born surpasses thought and speech.
The second best is to have seen the light
And then to go back quickly whence we came.
The feathery follies of his youth once over,
What trouble is beyond the range of man?
What heavy burden will he not endure?
Jealousy, faction, quarreling, and battle—
The bloodiness of war, the grief of war.
And in the end he comes to strengthless age,
Abhorred by all men, without company,

Unfriended in that uttermost twilight
Where he must live with every bitter thing.

This is the truth, not for me only,
But for this blind and ruined man.
Think of some shore in the north
Concussive waves make stream
This way and that in the gales of winter:
It is like that with him:
The wild wrack breaking over him
From head to foot, and coming on forever;
Now from the plunging down of the sun,
Now from the sunrise quarter,
Now from where the noonday gleams,
Now from the night and the north.

> [ANTIGONE *and* ISMENE *have been looking
> off-stage, left.* ANTIGONE *turns.*

⋖§ SCENE VI

ANTIGONE:

I think I see the stranger near us now,
And no man with him, father; but his eyes
Swollen with weeping as he comes.

> [POLYNEICES *enters, left.*

OEDIPUS:

Who comes?

ANTIGONE:

The one whom we have had so long in mind;
It is he who stands here; it is Polyneicês.

POLYNEICES:

Ah, now what shall I do? Sisters, shall I
Weep for my misfortunes or for those
I see in the old man, my father,
Whom I have found here in an alien land,
With two frail girls, an outcast for so long,
And with such garments! The abominable
Filth grown old with him, rotting his sides!
And on his sightless face the ragged hair
Streams in the wind. There's the same quality
In the food he carries for his thin old belly.
All this I learn too late.
And I swear now that I have been villainous
In not supporting you! You need not wait
To hear it said by others!
                  Only, think:
Compassion limits even the power of God;
So may there be a limit for you, father!
For all that has gone wrong may still be healed,
And surely the worst is passed!

Why are you silent?
Speak to me, father! Don't turn away from me!
Will you not answer me at all? Will you
Send me away without a word?
                  Not even
Tell me why you are enraged against me?

Daughters of Oedipus, my own sisters,
Try to move your so implacable father;
Do not let him reject me in such contempt!
Make him reply!
                I am here on pilgrimage. . . .

ANTIGONE:

    Poor brother: you yourself must tell him why.
    As men speak on they may sometimes give pleasure,
    Sometimes annoy, or sometimes touch the heart;
    And so somehow provide the mute with voices.

POLYNEICES:

    I will speak out then; your advice is fair.
    First, however, I must claim the help
    Of that same god, Poseidon, from whose altars
    The governor of this land has lifted me
    And sent me here, giving me leave to speak
    And to await response, and a safe passage.
    These are the favors I desire from you,
    Stranger, and from my sisters and my father.

    And now, father, I will tell you why I came.
    I am a fugitive, driven from my country,
    Because I thought fit, as the eldest born,
    To take my seat upon your sovereign throne.
    For that, Eteoclês, the younger of us,
    Banished me—but not by a decision
    In argument or ability or arms;
    Merely because he won the city over.
    Of this I believe the Furies that pursue you
    Were indeed the cause: and so I hear
    From clairvoyants whom I afterwards consulted.

    Then, when I went into the Dorian land,
    I took Adrastus as my father-in-law,
    And bound to me by oath whatever men
    Were known as leaders or as fighters there;
    My purpose being to form an expedition
    Of seven troops of spearmen against Thebes.—
    With which enlistment may I die for justice
    Or else expel the men who exiled me!

So it is. Then why should I come here now?
Father, my prayers must be made to you!
Mine and those of all who fight with me!
Their seven columns under seven captains
Even now complete the encirclement of Thebes:
Men like Amphiareus, the hard spear thrower,
Expert in spears and in the ways of eagles;
Second is Tydeus, the Aetolian,
Son of Oeneus; third is Eteoclus,
Born in Argos; fourth is Hippomedon
(His father, Talaus, sent him); Capaneus,
The fifth, has sworn he'll raze the town of Thebes
With fire-brands; and sixth is Parthenopaeus,
An Arcadian who roused himself to war—
Son of that virgin famous in the old time
Who long years afterward conceived and bore him—
Parthenopaeus, Atalanta's son.
And it is I, your son—or if I am not
Truly your son, since evil fathered me,
At least I am called your son—it is I who lead
The fearless troops of Argos against Thebes.

Now in the name of these two children, father,
And for your own soul's sake, we all implore
And beg you to give up your heavy wrath
Against me! I go forth to punish him,
The brother who robbed me of my fatherland!
If we can put any trust in oracles,
They say that those you bless shall come to power.

Now by the gods and fountains of our people,
I pray you, listen and comply! Are we not beggars
Both of us, and exiles, you and I?
We live by paying court to other men;
The same fate follows us.
But as for him—how insupportable!—
He lords it in our house, luxuriates there,
Laughs at us both!

If you will stand by me in my resolve,
I'll waste no time or trouble whipping him;
And then I'll re-establish you at home,
And settle there myself, and throw him out.
If your will is the same as mine, it's possible
To promise this. If not, I can't be saved.

CHORUS:

For the sake of the one who sent him, Oedipus,
Speak to this man before you send him back.

OEDIPUS:

Yes, gentlemen: but were it not Theseus,
The sovereign of your land, who sent him here,
Thinking it right that he should have an answer,
You never would have heard a sound from me.

Well: he has asked, and he shall hear from me
A kind of answer that will not overjoy him.
You scoundrel!
          When it was you who held
Throne and authority—as your brother now
Holds them in Thebes—you drove me into exile:
Me, your own father: made me a homeless man,
Insuring me these rags you maunder over
When you behold them now—now that you, too,
Have fallen on evil days and are in exile.

Weeping is no good now. However long
My life may last, I have to see it through;
But I regard you as a murderer!
For you reduced me to this misery,
You made me an alien. Because of you
I have begged my daily bread from other men.
If I had not these children to sustain me,
I might have lived or died for all your interest.

But they have saved me, they are my support,
And are not girls, but men, in faithfulness.
As for you two, you are no sons of mine!

And so it is that there are eyes that watch you
Even now; though not as they shall watch
If those troops are in fact marching on Thebes.
You cannot take that city. You'll go down
All bloody, and your brother, too.
                    For I
Have placed that curse upon you before this,
And now I invoke that curse to fight for me,
That you may see a reason to respect
Your parents, though your birth was as it was;
And though I am blind, not to dishonor me.
These girls did not.

And so your supplication and your throne
Are overmastered surely,—if accepted
Justice still has place in the laws of God.
Now go! For I abominate and disown you!
Wretched scum! Go with the malediction
I here pronounce for you: that you shall never
Master your native land by force of arms,
Nor ever see your home again in Argos,
The land below the hills; but you shall die
By your own brother's hand, and you shall kill
The brother who banished you. For this I pray.
And I cry out to the hated underworld
That it may take you home; cry out to those
Powers indwelling here; and to that Power
Of furious War that filled your hearts with hate!

Now you have heard me. Go: tell it to Thebes,
Tell all the Thebans; tell your faithful fighting
Friends what sort of honors
Oedipus has divided between his sons!

CHORUS:

Polyneicês, I find no matter for sympathy
In your directing yourself here. You may
Retire.

POLYNEICES:

Ah, what a journey! What a failure!
My poor companions! See the finish now
Of all we marched from Argos for! See me . . .
For I can neither speak of this to anyone
Among my friends, nor lead them back again;
I must go silently to meet this doom.

O sisters—daughters of his, sisters of mine!
You heard the hard curse of our father:
For God's sweet sake, if father's curse comes true,
And if you find some way to return home,
Do not, at least, dishonor me in death!
But give me a grave and what will quiet me.
Then you shall have, besides the praise he now
Gives you for serving him, an equal praise
For offices you shall have paid my ghost.

ANTIGONE:

Polyneicês, I beseech you, listen to me!

POLYNEICES:

Dearest—what is it? Tell me, Antigonê.

ANTIGONE:

Withdraw your troops to Argos as soon as you can.
Do not go to your own death and your city's!

POLYNEICES:

But that is impossible. How could I command
That army, even backward, once I faltered?

ANTIGONE:

Now why, boy, must your anger rise again?
What is the good of laying waste your homeland?

POLYNEICES:

It is shameful to run; and it is also shameful
To be a laughing-stock to a younger brother.

ANTIGONE:

But see how you fulfill his prophecies!
Did he not cry that you should kill each other?

POLYNEICES:

He wishes that. But I cannot give way.

ANTIGONE:

Ah, I am desolate! But who will dare
Go with you, after hearing the prophecies?

POLYNEICES:

I'll not report this trifle. A good commander
Tells heartening news, or keeps the news to himself.

ANTIGONE:

Then you have made up your mind to this, my
        brother?

POLYNEICES:

Yes. And do not try to hold me back.
The dark road is before me; I must take it,
Doomed by my father and his avenging Furies.
God bless you if you do what I have asked:
It is only in death that you can help me now.
Now let me go. Good-bye! You will not ever
Look in my eyes again.

ANTIGONE:

                        You break my heart!

POLYNEICES:

Do not grieve for me.

ANTIGONE:

Who would not grieve for you,
Sweet brother! You go with open eyes to death!

POLYNEICES:

Death, if that must be.

ANTIGONE:

No! Do as I ask!

POLYNEICES:

You ask the impossible.

ANTIGONE:

Then I am lost,
If I must be deprived of you!

POLYNEICES:

All that
Rests with the powers that are over us,—
Whether it must be so or otherwise.
You two—I pray no evil comes to you,
For all men know you merit no more pain.

[POLYNEICES *goes out, left. There is a dead
silence; then the* CHORUS *meditates.*

◄§ CHORAL POEM AND DIALOGUE

CHORUS:

So in this new event we see
New forms of terror working through the blind,
Or else inscrutable destiny.

I am not one to say "This is in vain"
Of anything allotted to mankind.
Though some must fall, or fall to rise again,
Time watches all things steadily—
                    [A terrific peal of thunder
Ah, Zeus! Heaven's height has cracked!
                        [Thunder and lightning

OEDIPUS:

O my child, my child! Could someone here—
Could someone bring the hero, Theseus?

ANTIGONE:

Father, what is your reason for calling him?

OEDIPUS:

God's beating thunder, any moment now,
Will clap me underground: send for him quickly!
                        [Thunder and lightning

CHORUS:

Hear it cascading down the air!
The god-thrown, the gigantic, holy sound!
Terror crawls to the tips of my hair!
My heart shakes!
                There the lightning flames again!
What heavenly marvel is it bringing 'round?
I fear it, for it never comes in vain,
But for man's luck or his despair. . . .
                        [Thunder and lightning

CHORUS:

Hear the wild thunder fall!
Towering Nature is transfixed!
Be merciful, great spirit, if you run
This sword of darkness through our mother land;
Come not for our confusion,
And deal no blows to me,
Though your tireless Furies stand
By him whom I have looked upon.
Great Zeus, I make my prayer to thee!

OEDIPUS:

Is the king near by? Will he come in time
To find me still alive, my mind still clear?

ANTIGONE:

Tell me what it is you have in mind!

OEDIPUS:

To give him now, in return for his great kindness,
The blessing that I promised I would give.
                                        [Thunder

CHORUS:

O noble son, return!
No matter if you still descend
In the deep fastness of the sea god's grove,
To make pure offering at his altar fire:
Come back quickly, for God's love!
Receive from this strange man
Whatever may be his heart's desire

That you and I and Athens are worthy of.
My lord, come quickly as you can!
[*The thunder continues, until it stops
abruptly with the entrance of* THESEUS,
left.

~§ SCENE VII

THESEUS:

Now why do you all together
Set up this shout once more?
I see it comes from you, as from our friend.
Is it a lightning bolt from Zeus? a squall
Of rattling hail? Those are familiar things
When such a tempest rages over heaven.

OEDIPUS:

My lord, I longed for you to come! This is
God's work, your lucky coming.

THESEUS:

Now, what new
Circumstance has arisen, son of Laius?

OEDIPUS:

My life sinks in the scale: I would not die
Without fulfilling what I promised Athens.

THESEUS:

What proof have you that your hour has come?

OEDIPUS:

The great, incessant thunder and continuous
Flashes of lightning from the hand of Zeus.

THESEUS:

> I believe you. I have seen you prophesy
> Many things, none falsely. What must be done?

OEDIPUS:

> I shall disclose to you, O son of Aegeus,
> What is appointed for you and for your city:
> A thing that age will never wear away.
> Presently now, without a soul to guide me,
> I'll lead you to the place where I must die;
> But you must never tell it to any man,
> Not even the neighborhood in which it lies.
> If you obey, this will count more for you
> Than many shields and many neighbors' spears.
> These things are mysteries, not to be explained;
> But you will understand when you come there
> Alone. Alone, because I cannot disclose it
> To any of your men or to my children,
> Much as I love and cherish them. But you
> Keep it secret always, and when you come
> To the end of life, then you must hand it on
> To your most cherished son, and he in turn
> Must teach it to his heir, and so forever.
> That way you shall forever hold this city
> Safe from the men of Thebes, the dragon's sons.
>
> For every nation that lives peaceably,
> There will be many others to grow hard
> And push their arrogance to extremes: the gods
> Attend to these things slowly. But they attend
> To those who put off God and turn to madness!
> You have no mind for that, child of Aegeus;
> Indeed, you know already all that I teach.
>
> Let us proceed then to that place
> And hesitate no longer; I am driven

By an insistent voice that comes from God.
Children, follow me this way: see, now
I have become your guide, as you were mine!
Come: do not touch me: let me alone discover
The holy and funereal ground where I
Must take this fated earth to be my shroud.

This way, O come! The angel of the dead,
Hermês, and veiled Persephonê lead me on!
            [*He leads them, firmly and slowly, to the
            left.*
O sunlight of no light! Once you were mine!
This is the last my flesh will feel of you;
For now I go to shade my ending day
In the dark underworld. Most cherished friend!
I pray that you and this your land and all
Your people may be blessed: remember me,
Be mindful of my death, and be
Fortunate in all the time to come!
            [OEDIPUS *goes out, followed by his chil
            dren and by* THESEUS *with his* SOLDIERS.
            The CHORUS *lifts its arms to pray.*

◄§ CHORAL POEM

CHORUS:

If I may dare to adore that Lady
The living never see,
And pray to the master of spirits plunged in night,
Who of vast Hell has sovereignty;
Let not our friend go down in grief and weariness
To that all-shrouding cold,
The dead men's plain, the house that has no light.

Because his sufferings were great, unmerited and un-
  told,
Let some just god relieve him from distress!

O powers under the earth, and tameless
Beast in the passage way,
Rumbler prone at the gate of the strange hosts,
Their guard forever, the legends say:
I pray you, even Death, offspring of Earth and Hell,
To let the descent be clear
As Oedipus goes down among the ghosts
On those dim fields of underground that all men liv-
  ing fear.
Eternal sleep, let Oedipus sleep well!
      [A *long pause. A* MESSENGER *comes in, left.*

◄§ SCENE VIII

MESSENGER:

Citizens, the briefest way to tell you
Would be to say that Oedipus is no more;
But what has happened cannot be told so simply—
It was no simple thing.

CHORUS:

                    He is gone, poor man?

MESSENGER:

You may be sure that he has left this world.

CHORUS:

By God's mercy, was his death a painless one?

MESSENGER:

That is the thing that seems so marvelous.

You know, for you were witnesses, how he
Left this place with no friend leading him,
Acting, himself, as guide for all of us.
Well, when he came to the steep place in the road,
The embankment there, secured with steps of brass,
He stopped in one of the many branching paths.

This was not far from the stone bowl that marks
Theseus' and Pirithous' covenant.

Half-way between that place of stone
With its hollow pear tree, and the marble tomb,
He sat down and undid his filthy garments;
Then he called his daughters and commanded
That they should bring him water from a fountain
For bathing and libation to the dead.
From there they saw the hillcrest of Demeter,
Freshener of all things: they ascended it
And soon came back with water for their father;
Then helped him properly to bathe and dress.

When everything was finished to his pleasure,
And no command of his remained undone,
Then the earth groaned with thunder from the god
    below;
And as they heard the sound, the girls shuddered,
And dropped to their father's knees, and began wail-
    ing,
Beating their breasts and weeping as if heartbroken.
And hearing them cry out so bitterly,
He put his arms around them, and said to them:

"Children, this day your father is gone from you.
All that was mine is gone. You shall no longer
Bear the burden of taking care of me—
I know it was hard, my children.—And yet one word
Frees us of all the weight and pain of life:

That word is love. Never shall you have more
From any man than you have had from me.
And now you must spend the rest of life without me."

That was the way of it. They clung together
And wept, all three. But when they finally stopped,
And no more sobs were heard, then there was
Silence, and in the silence suddenly
A voice cried out to him—of such a kind
It made our hair stand up in panic fear:
Again and again the call came from the god:
"Oedipus! Oedipus! Why are we waiting?
You delay too long; you delay too long to go!"

Then, knowing himself summoned by the spirit,
He asked that the lord Theseus come to him;
And when he had come, said: "O my prince and
        friend,
Give your right hand now as a binding pledge
To my two daughters; children, give him your hands.
Promise that you will never willingly
Betray them, but will carry out in kindness
Whatever is best for them in the days to come."

And Theseus swore to do it for his friend,
With such restraint as fits a noble king.
And when he had done so, Oedipus at once
Laid his blind hands upon his daughters, saying:
"Children, you must show your nobility,
And have the courage now to leave this spot.
You must not wish to see what is forbidden,
Or hear what may not afterward be told.
But go—go quickly. Only the lord Theseus
May stay to see the thing that now begins."

This much every one of us heard him say,
And then we came away with the sobbing girls.
But after a little while as we withdrew

We turned around—and nowhere saw that man,
But only the king, his hands before his face,
Shading his eyes as if from something fearful,
Awesome and unendurable to see.
Then very quickly we saw him do reverence
To Earth and to the powers of the air,
With one address to both.
                              But in what manner
Oedipus perished, no one of mortal men
Could tell but Theseus. It was not lightning,
Bearing its fire from Zeus, that took him off;
No hurricane was blowing.
But some attendant from the train of Heaven
Came for him; or else the underworld
Opened in love the unlit door of earth.
For he was taken without lamentation,
Illness or suffering; indeed his end
Was wonderful if mortal's ever was.

Should someone think I speak intemperately,
I make no apology to him who thinks so.

CHORUS:

But where are his children and the others with them?

MESSENGER:

They are not far away; the sound of weeping
Should tell you now that they are coming here.
                    [ANTIGONE *and* ISMENE *enter together.*

◆§ CHORAL DIALOGUE

ANTIGONE:

Now we may weep, indeed.
Now, if ever, we may cry

In bitter grief against our fate,
Our heritage still unappeased.
In other days we stood up under it,
Endured it for his sake,
The unrelenting horror. Now the finish
Comes, and we know only
In all that we have seen and done
Bewildering mystery.

CHORUS:

What happened?

ANTIGONE:

We can only guess, my friends.

CHORUS:

He has gone?

ANTIGONE:

He has; as one could wish him to.
Why not? It was not war
Nor the deep sea that overtook him,
But something invisible and strange
Caught him up—or down—
Into a space unseen.
But we are lost. A deathly
Night is ahead of us.
For how, in some far country wandering,
Or on the lifting seas,
Shall we eke out our lives?

ISMENE:

I cannot guess. But as for me
I wish that charnel Hell would take me
In one death with our father.
This is such desolation
I cannot go on living.

CHORUS:

>Most admirable sisters:
>Whatever God has brought about
>Is to be borne with courage.
>You must not feed the flames of grief.
>No blame can come to you.

ANTIGONE:

>One may long for the past
>Though at the time indeed it seemed
>Nothing but wretchedness and evil.
>Life was not sweet, yet I found it so
>When I could put my arms around my father.
>O father! O my dear!
>Now you are shrouded in eternal darkness,
>Even in that absence
>You shall not lack our love,
>Mine and my sister's love.

CHORUS:

>He lived his life.

ANTIGONE:

>He did as he had wished!

CHORUS:

>What do you mean?

ANTIGONE:

>In this land among strangers
>He died where he chose to die.
>He has his eternal bed well shaded,
>And in his death is not unmourned.
>My eyes are blind with tears
>From weeping for you, father.

The terror and the loss
Cannot be quieted.
I know you wished to die in a strange country,
Yet your death was so lonely!
Why could I not be with you?

ISMENE:

O pity! What is left for me?
What destiny awaits us both
Now we have lost our father?

CHORUS:

Dear children, remember
That his last hour was free and blessed.
So make an end of grieving!
Is anyone in all the world
Safe from unhappiness?

ANTIGONE:

Let us run back there!

ISMENE:

Why, what shall we do?

ANTIGONE:

I am carried away with longing—

ISMENE:

For what,—tell me!

ANTIGONE:

To see the resting place in the earth—

ISMENE:

Of whom?

ANTIGONE:

Father's! O what misery I feel!

ISMENE:

But that is not permitted. Do you not see?

ANTIGONE:

Do not rebuke me!

ISMENE:

—And remember, too—

ANTIGONE:

Oh, what?

ISMENE:

He had no tomb, there was no one near!

ANTIGONE:

Take me there and you can kill me, too!

ISMENE:

Ah! I am truly lost!
Helpless and so forsaken!
Where shall I go and how shall I live?

CHORUS:

You must not fear, now.

ANTIGONE:

Yes, but where is a refuge?

CHORUS:

A refuge has been found—

ANTIGONE:

Where do you mean?

CHORUS:

A place where you will be unharmed!

ANTIGONE:

No . . .

CHORUS:

What are you thinking?

ANTIGONE:

I think there is no way
For me to get home again.

CHORUS:

Do not go home!

ANTIGONE:

My home is in trouble.

CHORUS:

So it has been before.

ANTIGONE:

There was no help for it then: but now it is worse.

CHORUS:

A wide and desolate world it is for you.

ANTIGONE:

Great God! What way is left me?
Do the powers that rule our lives
Still press me on to hope at all?
                    [THESEUS *comes in, with attendants.*

THESEUS:

Mourn no more, children. Those to whom
The night of earth gives benediction
Should not be mourned. Retribution comes.

ANTIGONE:

Theseus: we fall on our knees to you

THESEUS:

What is it that you desire, children?

ANTIGONE:

We wish to see the place ourselves
In which our father rests.

THESEUS:

                     No, no.
It is not permissible to go there.

ANTIGONE:

My lord and ruler of Athens, why?

THESEUS:

Because your father told me, children,
That no one should go near the spot,
No mortal man should tell of it,
Since it is holy, and is his.
And if I kept this pledge, he said,
I should preserve my land from its enemies.
I swore I would, and the god heard me:
The oathkeeper who makes note of all.

ANTIGONE:

If this was our father's cherished wish,
We must be satisfied.
Send us back, then, to ancient Thebes,
And we may stop the bloody war
From coming between our brothers!

THESEUS:

I will do that, and whatever else
I am able to do for your happiness,
For his sake who has gone just now
Beneath the earth. I must not fail.

CHORUS:

Now let the weeping cease;
Let no one mourn again.
These things are in the hands of God

◆§ COMMENTARY

I. The profound myth of Oedipus gave Sophocles material for three plays: *Oedipus the King, Oedipus at Colonus,* and *Antigonê.* Unlike the *Oresteia* of Aeschylus, they were composed and produced independently of each other; but like the *Oresteia* they form a coherent trilogy. Though less familiar nowadays than the other two, *Oedipus at Colonus* has perhaps more significance and is no less beautiful. It completes the tale of Oedipus' life, and immediately precedes the action of *Antigonê.*

For those who do not read Greek, good English renderings of Sophocles are rare. Likely to be most available are the translations made forty years ago by R. C. Jebb. They are painstaking but give little or no idea of the quality of the originals.

II. The familiar art of the theater was once a discovery, and this discovery took place not long before Sophocles began to write. His older contemporary, Aeschylus, was credited by Aristotle with having been the first dramatic poet to use a second actor. The dramaturgy—though not the poetry—of Sophocles therefore emerged immediately from what we should call the archaic. We may justly admire the extent of its emergence. The Greek drama as Sophocles found it stood to previous Greek entertainment somewhat as the movies of our century stand to the art of the stage. His work might perhaps be compared with that of the director, Eisenstein, for he mastered and intelligently extended a new medium.

The two main elements in cinema are the art of the stage and the arts of mechanical reproduction. The two main elements in Greek drama were the national religious ritual, composed of singing, dancing and spectacle, and the national entertainment of epic recital. How these elements came to be joined is conjectural. It is known that professional men called rhapsodes had for centuries recited the Homeric stories, and, considering the many lively speeches in Homer, it is probable that these rhapsodes were skillful mimics. It may well have occurred to someone six centuries B.C. to employ the arts of story-telling and mimicry to enhance the choral dithyrambs at the Dionysian festival. A certain dancer would imitate a leading character of the song; the rest of the chorus would exchange verses with him. So, possibly, it began. A century later Greek drama had developed into the "miming of an action" and had become, undoubtedly, very exciting. A mere one-man narrative about Agamemnon or Oedipus had been enthralling enough to the Athenians; now they had a representation in which the events themselves, the heroes themselves, were set in motion before their eyes.

III. Aristotle, who particularly admired Sophocles' work, bears witness to the power of Greek tragedy in his time. And Aristotle said, among other things more open to misinterpretation, that the quality of a tragedy could be discovered as well by reading it as by going to see it produced. This should be a comfort to us, and we may add that so far as Greek plays are concerned, reading is nowadays a somewhat safer approach. Attempts have been made to reproduce the Greek amphitheater and what took place in it, but in English, for an audience reasonably robust, they have been in most cases perilous exhibitions. The nature of Greek dancing and choral singing is so obscure that they cannot be reconstructed with any certainty; nor, if they could, would there be much point in the reconstruction. These were arts that flourished in a religious atmosphere and for religious purposes that no longer exist.

For all the vigor of The Dance in our period, I should fear the effect of my choreography on the unity of a Greek play in performance. As for the singing, more is perhaps possible. In the Abbey Theatre production of Yeats's *Oedipus the King*, the choruses were chanted by singers trained in Gregorian music, and the effect is said to have been impressive. Yet, since I have no trustworthy theater or singing group in mind, I have left this version of *Oedipus at Colonus* almost bare of suggestions for its production; and I have called the choruses choral poems, thinking that if the play were staged it would be luck enough to have them well spoken.

It may be, indeed, that radio is the most nearly satisfactory means of presenting a Greek play to a modern audience. It is easy to see that such a manner of presentation, appealing wholly to the ear and imagination, avoids the difficulties of costuming and staging that must plague any stage performance.

IV. *Oedipus at Colonus* is reckoned on ancient authority to have been the last of more than one hundred plays by its author. It was composed probably in 406 B.C., when Sophocles was eighty-nine years old. Some of the play's peculiar interest lies in this fact, and in various matters implied by this fact. At the time of its composition the Peloponnesian War between Athens and Sparta had been in progress for more than a quarter of a century. To Colonus, where he was born, and to the great and hard-pressed city of which he was a beloved citizen, Sophocles paid his tribute in this play. Though Athens was still undefeated her lands had already been laid waste, and the verses about the olive trees may well have moved their first readers or auditors to tears. The play was not produced in the theater until 401 B.C., four years after the death of Sophocles and three years after the starvation and capitulation of Athens. *Oedipus at Colonus* is therefore one of the last considerable works known to us from the period of Athenian genius.

Like the six other extant plays of Sophocles, it is the work of a mind in the highest degree orderly, penetrating and sensitive, an enlightened mind aware of the moral issues in human action, and a reverent mind aware of the powers that operate through time and fortune on human affairs. But it is first of all the work of an artist, a maker of plots and poetry, and it is only from the ever-ambiguous expression of art that we may divine his thought or his theme. Accordingly we have here no such lucid a revelation of Athenian intellect as we find in the history of Thucydides or the dialogues of Plato. For its original audience the play shimmered with implications that are lost to us. Yet even we cannot fail to see in it the last, long reach toward truth of an artist who was formed by his great epoch and who perfectly represents it.

It would be hard to imagine any tribulation more severe than that endured by Oedipus, king of Thebes. At the summit of his power he discovered himself damned, by his own pertinacity discovered that he had horribly offended against the decencies by which men must live. In one day he fell from sovereignty and fame to self-blinded degradation, and later he was driven into exile. He comes on the stage a blind beggar led by a girl. The Athenians had no romantic notions about vagabondage or exile; in their eyes Oedipus had been reduced to the worst extremity, barring slavery, that a noble man could suffer.

But the atmosphere of the place to which the old

man comes is an atmosphere of shadiness, blessedness
and peace; and the contrast between Oedipus in his
rags and the beauty of Colonus is an effect of which
we are at once aware, an effect not unlike that of
Odysseus' awakening in the pretty island of Phaeacia.
Only here the poet's purposes are not so simple. For
this is a grove sacred to the Furies, and the Furies are
those spirits of retribution by whom sinners, murderers
especially, and Oedipus in particular, have been pursued.
It is furthermore well known to Sophocles' audience
that in the *Eumenidês* of Aeschylus, years before, these
spirits were persuaded by Athena to reconcile themselves to the superior rule of Athenian law. Thus gentled,
so to speak, in Attica, they have nevertheless great in-
trinsic power, and must be treated with tact. And they
are indeed, as we see here symbolized, the divinities
with whom Oedipus must make his peace.

To the sentimentalist there may be something odd
in the character and demeanor of this old man whom
adversity might properly have purged into sweetness and
resignation. His fund of both these qualities is limited.
The dignity of Oedipus is never in doubt, but observe
that this dignity is not of the sort associated with pa-
triarchs. It is not incompatible with a scornful and art-
ful wit, nor with a sort of fighting alertness: witness his
persuasive remarks to the Attic elders who try to dis-
miss him from the grove. Nor is it incompatible with
a definite savagery. The quick anger in which he killed
his father and goaded Teiresias, long ago, into telling
him the truth—it is, if anything, fiercer in his old age.
A literal thirst for blood appears in his prophecy
to Theseus of war between Thebes and Athens, and this
primitivism in Oedipus is all the more evident by contrast with the calm Athenian hero. Against Creon and
against his son he becomes a tower of passion and dis-
gust.

In what, then, is his dignity? Why is he not merely

an obsessed and vindictive old man? It should be remembered that one of Oedipus' distinguishing qualities was, in the first place, his intelligence. He saved Thebes once by solving the riddle of the Sphinx. He saved the city again by solving with furious persistence the riddle of his own birth. And in this play we see once more the working of that intellect, driving this time toward a transcendence of the purely human. During the years in which Oedipus has probed his own guilt he has come to terms with it. Though innocent of willful murder or incest, he has made expiation for what he recognized as his share of responsibility in those acts. Without reference to Freud we may perceive that in this whole fable of Oedipus the great poet is giving us to understand that the nature of man is darker than men believe it to be. Yet Oedipus is not penitent, for he has also recognized that the powers controlling life have, in a sense, chosen him as their example and instrument.

Thus it is not alone through passive suffering that the spirit of Oedipus attains power and blessedness. His rage and sternness in his last hours are the means of an affirmation, the most profound this poet could make. We recognize Oedipus' right to pass sentence on Creon and on his son, though by our first and easy standards neither would seem to deserve the curse pronounced on him. Creon is tricky and heartless, but he is "obeying the command of the State"; Polyneicês has been thoughtless of his father and fiercely jealous of his brother, but he does not seem a bad young man. In the larger context of Oedipus' fate, however, we may discern that their sins of meanness, of avarice, of irreverence, are no less grave than the sins of passion for which Oedipus was punished: that in condemning them to the merciless justice soon to descend, Oedipus acts thoroughly in accord with a moral order which his own experience has enabled him to understand.

And this may clarify for us the beautiful ending of the play. Oedipus has indeed endured his suffering with courage, but it is not until he has acted, and acted as the agent of divine justice, that the passionate man is fit to embody and to symbolize human divinity. Only then the Furies stand at his side; only then the gods receive him. And only then is bitterness lifted from him. His farewell to his daughters is the final word of Oedipus and of the tragedian. For, as a great Polish writer has written, "suffering is the lot of man, but not inevitable failure or worthless despair which is without end—suffering, the mark of manhood, which bears within its pain a hope of felicity like a jewel set in iron. . . ."

V. The quality of Sophocles cannot be rendered in the English of the King James Bible. Neither can it be rendered in the English of Bernard Shaw, of Maxwell Anderson or of Philip Barry. Rendered well, it would seem equally acceptable English to Jonathan Swift and to Ernest Hemingway. It can be exactly rendered only in what might be called the English of Sophocles. This requisite furnishes the translator with the fascination of what is, strictly speaking, impossible. I am merely prepared to assure the reader that this version is not a paraphrase or an adaptation, and that it is intended above all as a just representation of the Greek. Except for one or two variant phrases, I have followed the Oxford text of Sophocles as edited in 1923 by A. C. Pearson, Regius Professor of Greek at the University of Cambridge.

VI. The main dialogue in Greek dramatic poetry was cast in a regular meter (iambic trimeter) which may be imagined as a sort of unrhymed Alexandrine. A formal meter, it was at the same time, by virtue of its quantitative and non-syllabic basis, more flexible and perhaps more expressive than the French Alexandrine. A line of six stresses or accents is possible in English, but for purposes of dramatic dialogue it is neither traditional nor appropriate, being slow and foreign to the natural rhythm of our speech. The five stress line has not these disadvantages, and it has furthermore been brought to great subtlety and expressive precision not only by the later Elizabethan poets but by writers in our own day. This therefore was the meter chosen for rendering the dialogue.

The style of Sophocles was smooth. It has been likened by a modern critic to a molten flow of language, fitting and revealing every contour of the meaning, with no words wasted and no words poured on for effect. To approximate such purity I have sought a spare but felicitous manner of speech, not common and not "elevated" either, except by force of natural eloquence. The Greek writer did not disdain plainness when plainness was appropriate—appropriate, that is, both dramatically and within a context of verse very brilliant, mellifluous and powerful. As in every highly inflected language, the Greek order of words was controlled, by its masters, for special purposes of emphasis and even of meaning; and such of these as I have been acute enough to grasp I have tried to bring out by a comparable phrasing or rhythm in English. This I hold to be part of the business of "literal" rendering.

The difficulties involved in translating Greek dialogue are easily tripled when it comes to translating a chorus. Here the ellipses and compressions possible to the inflected idiom are particularly in evidence; and in the chorus, too, the poet concentrates his allusive power. For the modern reader, who has very little "literature" in the sense in which Samuel Johnson used the term,

two out of three allusions in the Greek odes will be
meaningless. This is neither surprising nor deplorable.
The Roman writer, Ennius, translating Euripides for a
Latin audience two centuries after the Periclean period,
found it advisable to omit many place names and to omit
or explain many mythological references; and his public
had greater reason to be familiar with such things than
we have. My handling of this problem has been governed
by the general wish to leave nothing in the English
that would drive the literate reader to a library. Two
examples should suffice.

On page 119, "the sea-surrounded west Where Pelop's
kin hold sway" is a translation of words whose
dictionary meaning is "the great Dorian island of
Pelops," in other words the Peloponnesus. The Greek
word for island which is Latinized as "nesus" was often
applied to bodies of land that we should not properly
define as islands. Hence "sea-surrounded" is a more exact
rendering here.

On page 137, "that torchlit Eleusinian shore": this
line and the following stanza refer to the holy shrine of
Eleusis, sacred to Demeter and Persephonê the goddess
of the underworld, where a ritual of communion and
revelation took place by torchlight every September. The
initiates in these rites were sworn to secrecy by priests
of an order called the Eumolpidae, or "sweet-voiced."
The shrine, partly subterranean, was on the rocky shore
of the bay of Eleusis behind the island of Salamis, about
fourteen miles northwest of Athens. It is not clear precisely what the Eleusinian mysteries consisted of, but it
is clear that they illuminated the life after death and
afforded great spiritual solace to the devout. Sophocles'
friend, Pericles, esteemed them of such importance to
the Athenian state that he rebuilt the shrine. Finally,
Eleusis was one of the places included in the "unifica-
tion of Attica" carried out, according to Athenian tradi-

tion, by Theseus. . . . I have tried to give the essential meaning and quality of this passage for readers who cannot be expected to have the foregoing information.

Rhyme as we know it was unknown to Greek poetry. Rhymed verse structures are much more remote from the Greek choral forms than iambic pentameter is from the iambic trimeter of their dialogue. And since it is desirable so far as possible to retain the character of the Greek poetry in the English, rhyme constitutes one of the farthest formal departures that we can make. Moreover, the artifice of rhyming draws the translator, irresistibly toward the addition of strokes of his own beyond the content or connotation of the text. Yet except by the use of rhymed stanzas and other formal devices of English verse, at least in certain instances, I do not see how the highly wrought regularity of the Sophoclean choruses, the lyricism deliberately distinct from dialogue, can be conveyed in untortured English. It has seemed to me necessary to convey these qualities, if possible; to convey them with the least possible increment of my own, but, when ingenuity should fail, to convey them even at the expense of absolute accuracy.

VII. This translation has been read in manuscript by two friends to whose scholarship and taste I am indebted for many suggestions: Associate Professor [now Professor] John H. Finley, Jr., of Harvard University, and Mr. Dudley Fitts. In collaborating with Mr. Fitts on two previous translations I learned most of what I know about rendering Greek poetry.

R. F.

March, 1941

As now reprinted, the translation has been revised or rewritten here and there. In some instances I have tried to render the Greek more closely, and in others I have had in mind a better level of style. I have allowed the Commentary to stand with but slight correction. It does not do justice to the poetry of Sophocles, but then neither does this, nor any other, translation.

R. F.

March, 1956

✎§ Antigone

AN ENGLISH VERSION
BY DUDLEY FITTS AND ROBERT FITZGERALD

TO HORACE GREGORY

πολλὰ γάρ σε θεσπίζονθ᾽ ὁρῶ
χοὐ ψευδόφημα

SCENE: *Before the palace of Creon, King of Thebes. A central double door, and two lateral doors. A platform extends the length of the façade, and from this platform three steps lead down into the "orchestra," or chorus-ground.* TIME: *dawn of the day after the repulse of the Argive army from the assault on Thebes.*

◂§ PROLOGUE

[ANTIGONE *and* ISMENE *enter from the central door of the Palace.*

ANTIGONE:

Ismenê, dear sister,
You would think that we had already suffered enough
For the curse on Oedipus:
I cannot imagine any grief
That you and I have not gone through. And now—

Have they told you of the new decree of our King
    Creon?

ISMENE:

I have heard nothing: I know
That two sisters lost two brothers, a double death
In a single hour; and I know that the Argive army
Fled in the night; but beyond this, nothing.

ANTIGONE:

I thought so. And that is why I wanted you
To come out here with me. There is something **we**
    must do.

ISMENE:

Why do you speak so strangely?

ANTIGONE:

Listen, Ismenê:
Creon buried our brother Eteoclês
With military honors, gave him a soldier's funeral,
And it was right that he should; but Polyneicês,
Who fought as bravely and died as miserably,—
They say that Creon has sworn
No one shall bury him, no one mourn for him,
But his body must lie in the fields, a sweet treasure
For carrion birds to find as they search for food.
That is what they say, and our good Creon is coming
    here
To announce it publicly; and the penalty—
Stoning to death in the public square!
                         There it is,
And now you can prove what you are:
A true sister, or a traitor to your family.

ISMENE:

Antigonê, you are mad! What could I possibly do?

ANTIGONE:

You must decide whether you will help me or not.

ISMENE:

I do not understand you. Help you in what?

ANTIGONE:

Ismenê, I am going to bury him. Will you come?

ISMENE:

Bury him! You have just said the new law forbids it.

ANTIGONE:

He is my brother. And he is your brother, too.

ISMENE:

But think of the danger! Think what Creon will do!

ANTIGONE:

Creon is not strong enough to stand in my way.

ISMENE:

Ah sister!
Oedipus died, everyone hating him
For what his own search brought to light, his eyes
Ripped out by his own hand; and Iocastê died,
His mother and wife at once: she twisted the cords
That strangled her life; and our two brothers died,
Each killed by the other's sword. And we are left:
But oh, Antigonê,
Think how much more terrible than these
Our own death would be if we should go against
     Creon
And do what he has forbidden! We are only women,

We cannot fight with men, Antigonê!
The law is strong, we must give in to the law
In this thing, and in worse. I beg the Dead
To forgive me, but I am helpless: I must yield
To those in authority. And I think it · is dangerous
    business
To be always meddling.

ANTIGONE:

                    If that is what you think,
I should not want you, even if you asked to come.
You have made your choice, you can be what you
    want to be.
But I will bury him; and if I must die,
I say that this crime is holy: I shall lie down
With him in death, and I shall be as dear
To him as he to me.
                    It is the dead,
Not the living, who make the longest demands:
We die for ever . . .
                    You may do as you like,
Since apparently the laws of the gods mean nothing
    to you.

ISMENE:

They mean a great deal to me; but I have no strength
To break laws that were made for the public good.

ANTIGONE:

That must be your excuse, I suppose. But as for me,
I will bury the brother I love.

ISMENE:

                              Antigonê,
I am so afraid for you!

ANTIGONE:

                         You need not be:
You have yourself to consider, after all.

ISMENE:

But no one must hear of this, you must tell no one!
I will keep it a secret, I promise!

ANTIGONE:

                         Oh tell it! Tell everyone!
Think how they'll hate you when it all comes out
If they learn that you knew about it all the time!

ISMENE:

So fiery! You should be cold with fear.

ANTIGONE:

Perhaps. But I am doing only what I must.

ISMENE:

But can you do it? I say that you cannot.

ANTIGONE:

Very well: when my strength gives out, I shall do no
      more.

ISMENE:

Impossible things should not be tried at all.

ANTIGONE:

Go away, Ismenê:
I shall be hating you soon, and the dead will too,
For your words are hateful. Leave me my foolish plan:
I am not afraid of the danger; if it means death,
It will not be the worst of deaths—death without
      honor.

ISMENE:

Go then, if you feel that you must.
You are unwise,
But a loyal friend indeed to those who love you.
        [*Exit into the Palace.* ANTIGONE *goes off,*
        L. Enter the CHORUS.

ᵉᵍ PÁRODOS

CHORUS:

Now the long blade of the sun, lying   [STROPHE 1
Level east to west, touches with glory
Thebes of the Seven Gates. Open, unlidded
Eye of golden day! O marching light
Across the eddy and rush of Dircê's stream,
Striking the white shields of the enemy
Thrown headlong backward from the blaze of morn-
    ing!

CHORAGOS:

Polyneicês their commander
Roused them with windy phrases,
He the wild eagle screaming
Insults above our land,
His wings their shields of snow,
His crest their marshalled helms.

CHORUS: [ANTISTROPHE 1

Against our seven gates in a yawning ring
The famished spears came onward in the night;
But before his jaws were sated with our blood,
Or pinefire took the garland of our towers,
He was thrown back; and as he turned, great Thebes—
No tender victim for his noisy power—
Rose like a dragon behind him, shouting war.

CHORAGOS:

For God hates utterly
The bray of bragging tongues;
And when he beheld their smiling,
Their swagger of golden helms,
The frown of his thunder blasted
Their first man from our walls.

CHORUS: [STROPHE 2

We heard his shout of triumph high in the air
Turn to a scream; far out in a flaming arc
He fell with his windy torch, and the earth struck
    him.
And others storming in fury no less than his
Found shock of death in the dusty joy of battle.

CHORAGOS:

Seven captains at seven gates
Yielded their clanging arms to the god
That bends the battle-line and breaks it.
These two only, brothers in blood,
Face to face in matchless rage,
Mirroring each the other's death,
Clashed in long combat.

CHORUS: [ANTISTROPHE 2

But now in the beautiful morning of victory
Let Thebes of the many chariots sing for joy!
With hearts for dancing we'll take leave of war:
Our temples shall be sweet with hymns of praise,
And the long night shall echo with our chorus.

⋙ SCENE I

CHORAGOS:

But now at last our new King is coming:
Creon of Thebes, Menoikeus' son.
In this auspicious dawn of his reign
What are the new complexities
That shifting Fate has woven for him?
What is his counsel? Why has he summoned
The old men to hear him?

> [*Enter* CREON *from the Palace, C. He addresses the* CHORUS *from the top step.*

CREON:

Gentlemen: I have the honor to inform you that our
Ship of State, which recent storms have threatened
to destroy, has come safely to harbor at last, guided
by the merciful wisdom of Heaven. I have summoned you here this morning because I know that
I can depend upon you: your devotion to King
Laïos was absolute; you never hesitated in your duty
to our late ruler Oedipus; and when Oedipus died,
your loyalty was transferred to his children. Unfortunately, as you know, his two sons, the princes
Eteoclês and Polyneicês, have killed each other in
battle; and I, as the next in blood, have succeeded
to the full power of the throne.
I am aware, of course, that no Ruler can expect complete loyalty from his subjects until he has been
tested in office. Nevertheless, I say to you at the
very outset that I have nothing but contempt for
the kind of Governor who is afraid, for whatever
reason, to follow the course that he knows is best
for the State; and as for the man who sets private

friendship above the public welfare,—I have no use
for him, either. I call God to witness that if I
saw my country headed for ruin, I should not be
afraid to speak out plainly; and I need hardly re-
mind you that I would never have any dealings with
an enemy of the people. No one values friendship
more highly than I; but we must remember that
friends made at the risk of wrecking our Ship are
not real friends at all.

These are my principles, at any rate, and that is why
I have made the following decision concerning the
sons of Oedipus: Eteoclês, who died as a man
should die, fighting for his country, is to be buried
with full military honors, with all the ceremony
that is usual when the greatest heroes die; but his
brother Polyneicês, who broke his exile to come
back with fire and sword against his native city and
the shrines of his fathers' gods, whose one idea was
to spill the blood of his blood and sell his own
people into slavery—Polyneicês, I say, is to have
no burial: no man is to touch him or say the least
prayer for him; he shall lie on the plain, unburied;
and the birds and the scavenging dogs can do with
him whatever they like.

This is my command, and you can see the wisdom
behind it. As long as I am King, no traitor is going
to be honored with the loyal man. But whoever
shows by word and deed that he is on the side of
the State,—he shall have my respect while he is
living, and my reverence when he is dead.

CHORAGOS:

If that is your will, Creon son of Menoîkeus,
You have the right to enforce it: we are yours.

CREON:

That is my will. Take care that you do your part.

CHORAGOS:

We are old men: let the younger ones carry it out.

CREON:

I do not mean that: the sentries have been appointed.

CHORAGOS:

Then what is it that you would have us do?

CREON:

You will give no support to whoever breaks this law.

CHORAGOS:

Only a crazy man is in love with death!

CREON:

And death it is; yet money talks, and the wisest
Have sometimes been known to count a few coins
    too many.
                  [*Enter* SENTRY *from L.*

SENTRY:

I'll not say that I'm out of breath from running, King,
    because every time I stopped to think about what
    I have to tell you, I felt like going back. And all
    the time a voice kept saying, "You fool, don't you
    know you're walking straight into trouble?"; and
    then another voice: "Yes, but if you let somebody
    else get the news to Creon first, it will be even worse
    than that for you!" But good sense won out, at
    least I hope it was good sense, and here I am with
    a story that makes no sense at all; but I'll tell it
    anyhow, because, as they say, what's going to hap-
    pen's going to happen, and—

CREON:

Come to the point. What have you to say?

SENTRY:

I did not do it. I did not see who did it. You must
not punish me for what someone else has done.

CREON:

A comprehensive defense! More effective, perhaps,
If I knew its purpose. Come: what is it?

SENTRY:

A dreadful thing . . . I don't know how to put it—

CREON:

Out with it!

SENTRY:

          Well, then;
The dead man—
          Polyneicês—
         [*Pause. The* SENTRY *is overcome, fumbles
for words.* CREON *waits impassively.*
          out there—
            someone,—
New dust on the slimy flesh!
         [*Pause. No sign from* CREON
Someone has given it burial that way, and
Gone . . .
         [*Long pause.* CREON *finally speaks with
deadly control:*

CREON:

And the man who dared do this?

SENTRY:

              I swear I
Do not know! You must believe me!
              Listen:
The ground was dry, not a sign of digging, no,

Not a wheeltrack in the dust, no trace of anyone.
It was when they relieved us this morning: and one
    of them,
The corporal, pointed to it.

                        There it was,
The strangest—
            Look:
The body, just mounded over with light dust: you see?
Not buried really, but as if they'd covered it
Just enough for the ghost's peace. And no sign
Of dogs or any wild animal that had been there.

And then what a scene there was! Every man of us
Accusing the other: we all proved the other man did
    it,
We all had proof that we could not have done it.
We were ready to take hot iron in our hands,
Walk through fire, swear by all the gods,
It was not I!
I do not know who it was, but it was not I!

            [CREON's *rage has been mounting steadily,*
            but the SENTRY *is too intent upon his story*
            to notice it
And then, when this came to nothing, someone said
A thing that silenced us and made us stare
Down at the ground: you had to be told the news,
And one of us had to do it! We threw the dice,
And the bad luck fell to me. So here I am,
No happier to be here than you are to have me:
Nobody likes the man who brings bad news.

CHORAGOS:

    I have been wondering, King: can it be that the gods
        have done this?

CREON: [*Furiously*

    Stop!
    Must you doddering wrecks

Go out of your heads entirely? "The gods!"
Intolerable!
The gods favor this corpse? Why? How had he
    served them?
Tried to loot their temples, burn their images,
Yes, and the whole State, and its laws with it!
Is it your senile opinion that the gods love to honor
    bad men?
A pious thought!—

                    No, from the very beginning
There have been those who have whispered together,
Stiff-necked anarchists, putting their heads together,
Scheming against me in alleys. These are the men,
And they have bribed my own guard to do this thing.

Money!   [*Sententiously*
There's nothing in the world so demoralizing as money.
Down go your cities,
Homes gone, men gone, honest hearts corrupted,
Crookedness of all kinds, and all for money!

                                    [*To* SENTRY
                                    But you—!
I swear by God and by the throne of God,
The man who has done this thing shall pay for it!
Find that man, bring him here to me, or your death
Will be the least of your problems: I'll string you up
Alive, and there will be certain ways to make you
Discover your employer before you die;
And the process may teach you a lesson you seem to
    have missed:
The dearest profit is sometimes all too dear:
That depends on the source. Do you understand me?
A fortune won is often misfortune.

SENTRY:

King, may I speak?

CREON:

                    Your very voice distresses me.

SENTRY:

Are you sure that it is my voice, and not your conscience?

CREON:

By God, he wants to analyze me now!

SENTRY:

It is not what I say, but what has been done, that hurts you.

CREON:

You talk too much.

SENTRY:

Maybe; but I've done nothing.

CREON:

Sold your soul for some silver: that's all you've done.

SENTRY:

How dreadful it is when the right judge judges wrong!

CREON:

Your figures of speech
May entertain you now; but unless you bring me the man,
You will get little profit from them in the end.
[Exit CREON *into the Palace.*

SENTRY:

"Bring me the man"—!
I'd like nothing better than bringing him the man!
But bring him or not, you have seen the last of me here.
At any rate, I am safe!
[Exit SENTRY

ᵕᶳ ODE I

CHORUS: [STROPHE 1

Numberless are the world's wonders, but none
More wonderful than man; the stormgray sea
Yields to his prows, the huge crests bear him high;
Earth, holy and inexhaustible, is graven
With shining furrows where his plows have gone
Year after year, the timeless labor of stallions.

[ANTISTROPHE 1

The lightboned birds and beasts that cling to cover,
The lithe fish lighting their reaches of dim water,
All are taken, tamed in the net of his mind;
The lion on the hill, the wild horse windy-maned,
Resign to him; and his blunt yoke has broken
The sultry shoulders of the mountain bull.

[STROPHE 2

Words also, and thought as rapid as air,
He fashions to his good use; statecraft is his,
And his the skill that deflects the arrows of snow,
The spears of winter rain: from every wind
He has made himself secure—from all but one:
In the late wind of death he cannot stand.

[ANTISTROPHE 2

O clear intelligence, force beyond all measure!
O fate of man, working both good and evil!
When the laws are kept, how proudly his city stands!
When the laws are broken, what of his city then?
Never may the anárchic man find rest at my hearth,
Never be it said that my thoughts are his thoughts.

⚜ SCENE II

[Re-enter SENTRY *leading* ANTIGONE.

CHORAGOS:

What does this mean? Surely this captive woman
Is the Princess, Antigonê. Why should she be taken?

SENTRY:

Here is the one who did it! We caught her
In the very act of burying him.—Where is Creon?

CHORAGOS:

Just coming from the house.

[Enter CREON, *C.*

CREON:

What has happened?
Why have you come back so soon?

SENTRY:

[Expansively
O King,
A man should never be too sure of anything:
I would have sworn
That you'd not see me here again: your anger
Frightened me so, and the things you threatened me
with;
But how could I tell then
That I'd be able to solve the case so soon?

No dice-throwing this time: I was only too glad to
come!

Here is this woman. She is the guilty one:
We found her trying to bury him.

Take her, then; question her; judge her as you will.
I am through with the whole thing now, and glád óf
    it.

CREON:

But this is Antigonê! Why have you brought her
    here?

SENTRY:

She was burying him, I tell you!

CREON: [*Severely*
                                    Is this the truth?

SENTRY:

I saw her with my own eyes. Can I say more?

CREON:

The details: come, tell me quickly!

SENTRY:

                                    It was like this:
After those terrible threats of yours, King,
We went back and brushed the dust away from the
    body.
The flesh was soft by now, and stinking,
So we sat on a hill to windward and kept guard.
No napping this time! We kept each other awake.
But nothing happened until the white round sun
Whirled in the center of the round sky over us:
Then, suddenly,
A storm of dust roared up from the earth, and the sky
Went out, the plain vanished with all its trees
In the stinging dark. We closed our eyes and endured
    it.
The whirlwind lasted a long time, but it passed;
And then we looked, and there was Antigonê!

I have seen
A mother bird come back to a stripped nest, heard
Her crying bitterly a broken note or two
For the young ones stolen. Just so, when this girl
Found the bare corpse, and all her love's work wasted,
She wept, and cried on heaven to damn the hands
That had done this thing.
                              And then she brought more dust
And sprinkled wine three times for her brother's ghost.

We ran and took her at once. She was not afraid,
Not even when we charged her with what she had
    done.
She denied nothing.
                         And this was a comfort to me,
And some uneasiness: for it is a good thing
To escape from death, but it is no great pleasure
To bring death to a friend.
                              Yet I always say
There is nothing so comfortable as your own safe skin!

CREON: [*Slowly, dangerously*

And you, Antigonê,
You with your head hanging,—do you confess this
    thing?

ANTIGONE:

I do. I deny nothing.

CREON: [*To* SENTRY:
                   You may go.

                                    [*Exit* SENTRY
                                    [*To* ANTIGONE:
Tell me, tell me briefly:
Had you heard my proclamation touching this matter?

ANTIGONE:

It was public. Could I help hearing it?

CREON:

And yet you dared defy the law.

ANTIGONE:

                        I dared.
It was not God's proclamation. That final Justice
That rules the world below makes no such laws.

Your edict, King, was strong,
But all your strength is weakness itself against
The immortal unrecorded laws of God.
They are not merely now: they were, and shall be,
Operative for ever, beyond man utterly.

I knew I must die, even without your decree:
I am only mortal. And if I must die
Now, before it is my time to die,
Surely this is no hardship: can anyone
Living, as I live, with evil all about me,
Think Death less than a friend? This death of mine
Is of no importance; but if I had left my brother
Lying in death unburied, I should have suffered.
Now I do not.
               You smile at me. Ah Creon,
Think me a fool, if you like; but it may well be
That a fool convicts me of folly.

CHORAGOS:

Like father, like daughter: both headstrong, deaf to
    reason!
She has never learned to yield.

CREON:

                  She has much to learn.
The inflexible heart breaks first, the toughest iron
Cracks first, and the wildest horses bend their necks

At the pull of the smallest curb.

Pride? In a slave?
This girl is guilty of a double insolence,
Breaking the given laws and boasting of it.
Who is the man here,
She or I, if this crime goes unpunished?
Sister's child, or more than sister's child,
Or closer yet in blood—she and her sister
Win bitter death for this!

[To servants:

Go, some of you,
Arrest Ismenê. I accuse her equally.
Bring her: you will find her sniffling in the house there.

Her mind's a traitor: crimes kept in the dark
Cry for light, and the guardian brain shudders;
But how much worse than this
Is brazen boasting of barefaced anarchy!

ANTIGONE:

Creon, what more do you want than my death?

CREON:

Nothing.
That gives me everything.

ANTIGONE:

Then I beg you: kill me.
This talking is a great weariness: your words
Are distasteful to me, and I am sure that mine
Seem so to you. And yet they should not seem so:
I should have praise and honor for what I have done.
All these men here would praise me
Were their lips not frozen shut with fear of you.

[Bitterly

Ah the good fortune of kings,
Licensed to say and do whatever they please!

CREON:

You are alone here in that opinion.

ANTIGONE:

No, they are with me. But they keep their tongues in leash.

CREON:

Maybe. But you are guilty, and they are not.

ANTIGONE:

There is no guilt in reverence for the dead.

CREON:

But Eteoclês—was he not your brother too?

ANTIGONE:

My brother too.

CREON:

And you insult his memory?

ANTIGONE: [Softly

The dead man would not say that I insult it.

CREON:

He would: for you honor a traitor as much as him.

ANTIGONE:

His own brother, traitor or not, and equal in blood.

CREON:

He made war on his country. Eteoclês defended it.

ANTIGONE:

Nevertheless, there are honors due all the dead.

CREON:

But not the same for the wicked as for the just.

ANTIGONE:

Ah Creon, Creon,
Which of us can say what the gods hold wicked?

CREON:

An enemy is an enemy, even dead.

ANTIGONE:

It is my nature to join in love, not hate.

CREON: [*Finally losing patience*

Go join them, then; if you must have your love,
Find it in hell!

CHORAGOS:

But see, Ismenê comes:
[*Enter* ISMENE, *guarded*
Those tears are sisterly, the cloud
That shadows her eyes rains down gentle sorrow.

CREON:

You too, Ismenê,
Snake in my ordered house, sucking my blood
Stealthily—and all the time I never knew
That these two sisters were aiming at my throne!
Ismenê,
Do you confess your share in this crime, or deny it?
Answer me.

ISMENE:

Yes, if she will let me say so. I am guilty.

ANTIGONE: [*Coldly*

No, Ismenê. You have no right to say so.
You would not help me, and I will not have you help
    me.

ISMENE:

But now I know what you meant; and I am here
To join you, to take my share of punishment.

ANTIGONE:

The dead man and the gods who rule the dead
Know whose act this was. Words are not friends.

ISMENE:

Do you refuse me, Antigonê? I want to die with you:
I too have a duty that I must discharge to the dead.

ANTIGONE:

You shall not lessen my death by sharing it.

ISMENE:

What do I care for life when you are dead?

ANTIGONE:

Ask Creon. You're always hanging on his opinions.

ISMENE:

You are laughing at me. Why, Antigonê?

ANTIGONE:

It's a joyless laughter, Ismenê.

ISMENE:

                          But can I do nothing?

ANTIGONE:

Yes. Save yourself. I shall not envy you.

There are those who will praise you; I shall have
    honor, too.

ISMENE:

But we are equally guilty!

ANTIGONE:

                  No more, Ismenê.
You are alive, but I belong to Death.

CREON: [*To the* CHORUS:

Gentlemen, I beg you to observe these girls:
One has just now lost her mind; the other,
It seems, has never had a mind at all.

ISMENE:

Grief teaches the steadiest minds to waver, King.

CREON:

Yours certainly did, when you assumed guilt with the
    guilty!

ISMENE:

But how could I go on living without her?

CREON:

                           You are.
She is already dead.

ISMENE:

               But your own son's bride!

CREON:

There are places enough for him to push his plow.
I want no wicked women for my sons!

ISMENE:

O dearest Haimon, how your father wrongs you!

CREON:

I've had enough of your childish talk of marriage!

CHORAGOS:

Do you really intend to steal this girl from your son?

CREON:

No; Death will do that for me.

CHORAGOS:

Then she must die?

CREON: [*Ironically*

You dazzle me.
                    —But enough of this talk!
                                                    [*To* GUARDS:
You, there, take them away and guard them well:
For they are but women, and even brave men run
When they see Death coming.
                    [*Exeunt* ISMENE, ANTIGONE, *and* GUARDS

❧ ODE II

CHORUS: [STROPHE 1

Fortunate is the man who has never tasted God's
        vengeance!
Where once the anger of heaven has struck, that
        house is shaken
For ever: damnation rises behind each child
Like a wave cresting out of the black northeast,
When the long darkness under sea roars up
And bursts drumming death upon the windwhipped
        sand.

[ANTISTROPHE 1

I have seen this gathering sorrow from time long past
Loom upon Oedipus' children: generation from generation
eration
Takes the compulsive rage of the enemy god.
So lately this last flower of Oedipus' line
Drank the sunlight! but now a passionate word
And a handful of dust have closed up all its beauty.

What mortal arrogance   [STROPHE 2
Transcends the wrath of Zeus?
Sleep cannot lull him, nor the effortless long months
Of the timeless gods: but he is young for ever,
And his house is the shining day of high Olympos.
All that is and shall be,
And all the past, is his.
No pride on earth is free of the curse of heaven.

The straying dreams of men   [ANTISTROPHE 2
May bring them ghosts of joy:
But as they drowse, the waking embers burn them;
Or they walk with fixed éyes, as blind men walk.
But the ancient wisdom speaks for our own time:
Fate works most for woe
With Folly's fairest show.
Man's little pleasure is the spring of sorrow.

◆§ SCENE III

CHORAGOS:

But here is Haimon, King, the last of all your sons.
Is it grief for Antigonê that brings him here,
And bitterness at being robbed of his bride?
[*Enter* HAIMON

CREON:

We shall soon see, and no need of diviners.
                                        —Son,
You have heard my final judgment on that girl:
Have you come here hating me, or have you come
With deference and with love, whatever I do?

HAIMON:

I am your son, father. You are my guide.
You make things clear for me, and I obey you.
No marriage means more to me than your continuing
    wisdom.

CREON:

Good. That is the way to behave: subordinate
Everything else, my son, to your father's will.
This is what a man prays for, that he may get
Sons attentive and dutiful in his house,
Each one hating his father's enemies,
Honoring his father's friends. But if his sons
Fail him, if they turn out unprofitably,
What has he fathered but trouble for himself
And amusement for the malicious?
                                        So you are right
Not to lose your head over this woman.
Your pleasure with her would soon grow cold, Hai-
    mon,
And then you'd have a hellcat in bed and elsewhere.
Let her find her husband in Hell!
Of all the people in this city, only she
Has had contempt for my law and broken it.

Do you want me to show myself weak before the
    people?
Or to break my sworn word? No, and I will not.
The woman dies.

I suppose she'll plead "family ties." Well, let her.
If I permit my own family to rebel,
How shall I earn the world's obedience?
Show me the man who keeps his house in hand,
He's fit for public authority.
                      I'll have no dealings
With law-breakers, critics of the government:
Whoever is chosen to govern should be obeyed—
Must be obeyed, in all things, great and small,
Just and unjust! O Haimon,
The man who knows how to obey, and that man only,
Knows how to give commands when the time comes.
You can depend on him, no matter how fast
The spears come: he's a good soldier, he'll stick it out.

Anarchy, anarchy! Show me a greater evil!
This is why cities tumble and the great houses rain
    down,
This is what scatters armies!

No, no: good lives are made so by discipline.
We keep the laws then, and the lawmakers,
And no woman shall seduce us. If we must lose,
Let's lose to a man, at least! Is a woman stronger than
    we?

CHORAGOS:

Unless time has rusted my wits,
What you say, King, is said with point and dignity.

HAIMON: *[Boyishly earnest*

Father:
Reason is God's crowning gift to man, and you are
    right
To warn me against losing mine. I cannot say—
I hope that I shall never want to say!—that you
Have reasoned badly. Yet there are other men

Who can reason, too; and their opinions might be
    helpful.
You are not in a position to know everything
That people say or do, or what they feel:
Your temper terrifies them—everyone
Will tell you only what you like to hear.
But I, at any rate, can listen; and I have heard them
Muttering and whispering in the dark about this girl.
They say no woman has ever, so unreasonably,
Died so shameful a death for a generous act:
"She covered her brother's body. Is this indecent?
She kept him from dogs and vultures. Is this a crime?
Death?—She should have all the honor that we can
    give her!"

This is the way they talk out there in the city.

You must believe me:
Nothing is closer to me than your happiness.
What could be closer? Must not any son
Value his father's fortune as his father does his?
I beg you, do not be unchangeable:
Do not believe that you alone can be right.
The man who thinks that,
The man who maintains that only he has the powei
To reason correctly, the gift to speak, the soul—
A man like that, when you know him, turns out
    empty.

It is not reason never to yield to reason!

In flood time you can see how some trees bend,
And because they bend, even their twigs are safe,
While stubborn trees are torn up, roots and all.
And the same thing happens in sailing:
Make your sheet fast, never slacken,—and over you
    go,
Head over heels and under: and there's your voyage.

Forget you are angry! Let yourself be moved!
I know I am young; but please let me say this:
The ideal condition
Would be, I admit, that men should be right by in-
stinct;
But since we are all too likely to go astray,
The reasonable thing is to learn from those who can
teach.

CHORAGOS:

You will do well to listen to him, King,
If what he says is sensible. And you, Haimon,
Must listen to your father.—Both speak well.

CREON:

You consider it right for a man of my years and experience
To go to school to a boy?

HAIMON:

                    It is not right
If I am wrong. But if I am young, and right,
What does my age matter?

CREON:

You think it right to stand up for an anarchist?

HAIMON:

Not at all. I pay no respect to criminals.

CREON:

Then she is not a criminal?

HAIMON:

The City would deny it, to a man.

CREON:

And the City proposes to teach me how to rule?

HAIMON:

Ah. Who is it that's talking like a boy now?

CREON:

My voice is the one voice giving orders in this City!

HAIMON:

It is no City if it takes orders from one voice.

CREON:

The State is the King!

HAIMON:

Yes, if the State is a desert.
[Pause

CREON:

This boy, it seems, has sold out to a woman.

HAIMON:

If you are a woman: my concern is only for you.

CREON:

So? Your "concern"! In a public brawl with your father!

HAIMON:

How about you, in a public brawl with justice?

CREON:

With justice, when all that I do is within my rights?

HAIMON:

You have no right to trample on God's right.

CREON: *[Completely out of control*

Fool, adolescent fool! Taken in by a woman!

HAIMON:

You'll never see me taken in by anything vile.

CREON:

Every word you say is for her!

HAIMON: [*Quietly, darkly*

                    And for you.
And for me. And for the gods under the earth.

CREON:

You'll never marry her while she lives.

HAIMON:

Then she must die.—But her death will cause another.

CREON:

Another?
Have you lost your senses? Is this an open threat?

HAIMON:

There is no threat in speaking to emptiness.

CREON:

I swear you'll regret this superior tone of yours!
You are the empty one!

HAIMON:

                              If you were not my father,
I'd say you were perverse.

CREON:

You girlstruck fool, don't play at words with me!

HAIMON:

I am sorry. You prefer silence.

CREON:

> Now, by God—!
> I swear, by all the gods in heaven above us,
> You'll watch it, I swear you shall!
>> [*To the* SERVANTS:
>> Bring her out!
> Bring the woman out! Let her die before his eyes!
> Here, this instant, with her bridegroom beside her!

HAIMON:

> Not here, no; she will not die here, King.
> And you will never see my face again.
> Go on raving as long as you've a friend to endure you.
>> [*Exit* HAIMON

CHORAGOS:

> Gone, gone.
> Creon, a young man in a rage is dangerous!

CREON:

> Let him do, or dream to do, more than a man can.
> He shall not save these girls from death.

CHORAGOS:

> These girls?
> You have sentenced them both?

CREON:

> No, you are right.
> I will not kill the one whose hands are clean.

CHORAGOS:

> But Antigonê?

CREON: [*Somberly*

        I will carry her far away
Out there in the wilderness, and lock her
Living in a vault of stone. She shall have food,
As the custom is, to absolve the State of her death.
And there let her pray to the gods of hell:
They are her only gods:
Perhaps they will show her an escape from death,
Or she may learn,
               though late,
That piety shown the dead is pity in vain.

                                   [*Exit* CREON

◆§ ODE III

CHORUS:

Love, unconquerable   [STROPHE
Waster of rich men, keeper
Of warm lights and all-night vigil
In the soft face of a girl:
Sea-wanderer, forest-visitor!
Even the pure Immortals cannot escape you,
And mortal man, in his one day's dusk,
Trembles before your glory.

Surely you swerve upon ruin   [ANTISTROPHE
The just man's consenting heart,
As here you have made bright anger
Strike between father and son—
And none has conquered but Love!
A girl's glánce wórking the will of heaven:
Pleasure to her alone who mocks us,
Merciless Aphroditê.

◆§ SCENE IV

CHORAGOS: [As ANTIGONE *enters guarded*

But I can no longer stand in awe of this,
Nor, seeing what I see, keep back my tears.
Here is Antigonê, passing to that chamber
Where all find sleep at last.

ANTIGONE:

Look upon me, friends, and pity me   [STROPHE 1
Turning back at the night's edge to say
Good-by to the sun that shines for me no longer;
Now sleepy Death
Summons me down to Acheron, that cold shore:
There is no bridesong there, nor any music.

CHORUS:

Yet not unpraised, not without a kind of honor,
You walk at last into the underworld;
Untouched by sickness, broken by no sword.
What woman has ever found your way to death?

ANTIGONE:

                                         [ANTISTROPHE 1
How often I have heard the story of Niobê,
Tantalos' wretched daughter, how the stone
Clung fast about her, ivy-close: and they say
The rain falls endlessly
And sifting soft snow; her tears are never done.
I feel the loneliness of her death in mine.

CHORUS:

But she was born of heaven, and you
Are woman, woman-born. If her death is yours,

A mortal woman's, is this not for you
Glory in our world and in the world beyond?

ANTIGONE:

You laugh at me. Ah, friends, friends,   [STROPHE 2
Can you not wait until I am dead? O Thebes,
O men many-charioted, in love with Fortune,
Dear springs of Dircê, sacred Theban grove,
Be witnesses for me, denied all pity,
Unjustly judged! and think a word of love
For her whose path turns
Under dark earth, where there are no more tears.

CHORUS:

You have passed beyond human daring and come at
    last
Into a place of stone where Justice sits.
I cannot tell
What shape of your father's guilt appears in this.

ANTIGONE:

                                [ANTISTROPHE 2
You have touched it at last: that bridal bed
Unspeakable, horror of son and mother mingling:
Their crime, infection of all our family!
O Oedipus, father and brother!
Your marriage strikes from the grave to murder mine.
I have been a stranger here in my own land:
All my life
The blasphemy of my birth has followed me.

CHORUS:

Reverence is a virtue, but strength
Lives in established law: that must prevail.
You have made your choice,
Your death is the doing of your conscious hand.

ANTIGONE:

[EPODE

Then let me go, since all your words are bitter,
And the very light of the sun is cold to me.
Lead me to my vigil, where I must have
Neither love nor lamentation; no song, but silence.

[CREON *interrupts impatiently*

CREON:

If dirges and planned lamentations could put off
    death,
Men would be singing for ever.

[*To the* SERVANTS:
Take her, go!
You know your orders: take her to the vault
And leave her alone there. And if she lives or dies,
That's her affair, not ours: our hands are clean.

ANTIGONE:

O tomb, vaulted bride-bed in eternal rock,
Soon I shall be with my own again
Where Persephonê welcomes the thin ghosts under-
    ground:
And I shall see my father again, and you, mother,
And dearest Polyneicês—

                    dearest indeed
To me, since it was my hand
That washed him clean and poured the ritual wine:
And my reward is death before my time!

And yet, as men's hearts know, I have done no wrong,
I have not sinned before God. Or if I have,
I shall know the truth in death. But if the guilt
Lies upon Creon who judged me, then, I pray,
May his punishment equal my own.

CHORAGOS:

                          O passionate heart,
Unyielding, tormented still by the same winds!

CREON:

Her guards shall have good cause to regret their delaying.

ANTIGONE:

Ah! That voice is like the voice of death!

CREON:

I can give you no reason to think you are mistaken.

ANTIGONE:

Thebes, and you my fathers' gods,
And rulers of Thebes, you see me now, the last
Unhappy daughter of a line of kings,
Your kings, led away to death. You will remember
What things I suffer, and at what men's hands,
Because I would not transgress the laws of heaven.
                        [*To the* GUARDS, *simply:*
Come: let us wait no longer.
                        [Exit ANTIGONE, *L.,* guarded

⛊ ODE IV

CHORUS:

All Danaë's beauty was locked away   [STROPHE 1
In a brazen cell where the sunlight could not come:
A small room, still as any grave, enclosed her.
Yet she was a princess too,
And Zeus in a rain of gold poured love upon her.
O child, child,

No power in wealth or war
Or tough sea-blackened ships
Can prevail against untiring Destiny!

[ANTISTROPHE 1

And Dryas' son also, that furious king,
Bore the god's prisoning anger for his pride:
Sealed up by Dionysos in deaf stone,
His madness died among echoes.
So at the last he learned what dreadful power
His tongue had mocked:
For he had profaned the revels,
And fired the wrath of the nine
Implacable Sisters that love the sound of the flute.

[STROPHE 2

And old men tell a half-remembered tale
Of horror done where a dark ledge splits the sea
And a double surf beats on the gráy shóres:
How a king's new woman, sick
With hatred for the queen he had imprisoned,
Ripped out his two sons' eyes with her bloody hands
While grinning Arês watched the shuttle plunge
Four times: four blind wounds crying for revenge,

[ANTISTROPHE 2

Crying, tears and blood mingled.—Piteously born,
Those sons whose mother was of heavenly birth!
Her father was the god of the North Wind
And she was cradled by gales,
She raced with young colts on the glittering hills
And walked untrammeled in the open light:
But in her marriage deathless Fate found means
To build a tomb like yours for all her joy.

⋖§ SCENE V

> [*Enter blind* TEIRESIAS, *led by a boy. The*
> *opening speeches of* TEIRESIAS *should be*
> *in singsong contrast to the realistic lines of*
> CREON.

TEIRESIAS:

This is the way the blind man comes, Princes, Princes,
Lock-step, two heads lit by the eyes of one.

CREON:

What new thing have you to tell us, old Teiresias?

TEIRESIAS:

I have much to tell you: listen to the prophet, Creon.

CREON:

I am not aware that I have ever failed to listen.

TEIRESIAS:

Then you have done wisely, King, and ruled well.

CREON:

I admit my debt to you. But what have you to say?

TEIRESIAS:

This, Creon: you stand once more on the edge of fate.

CREON:

What do you mean? Your words are a kind of dread.

TEIRESIAS:

Listen, Creon:
I was sitting in my chair of augury, at the place

Where the birds gather about me. They were all
    a-chatter,
As is their habit, when suddenly I heard
A strange note in their jangling, a scream, a
Whirring fury; I knew that they were fighting,
Tearing each other, dying
In a whirlwind of wings clashing. And I was afraid.
I began the rites of burnt-offering at the altar,
But Hephaistos failed me: instead of bright flame,
There was only the sputtering slime of the fat thigh-
    flesh
Melting: the entrails dissolved in gray smoke,
The bare bone burst from the welter. And no blaze!

This was a sign from heaven. My boy described it,
Seeing for me as I see for others.

I tell you, Creon, you yourself have brought
This new calamity upon us. Our hearths and altars
Are stained with the corruption of dogs and carrion
    birds
That glut themselves on the corpse of Oedipus' son.
The gods are deaf when we pray to them, their fire
Recoils from our offering, their birds of omen
Have no cry of comfort, for they are gorged
With the thick blood of the dead.
                                    O my son,
These are no trifles! Think: all men make mistakes,
But a good man yields when he knows his course is
    wrong,
And repairs the evil. The only crime is pride.

Give in to the dead man, then: do not fight with a
    corpse—
What glory is it to kill a man who is dead?
Think, I beg you:
It is for your own good that I speak as I do.
You should be able to yield for your own good.

CREON:

It seems that prophets have made me their especial
    province.
All my life long
I have been a kind of butt for the dull arrows
Of doddering fortune-tellers!
                                No, Teiresias:
If your birds—if the great eagles of God himself
Should carry him stinking bit by bit to heaven,
I would not yield. I am not afraid of pollution:
No man can defile the gods.
                                Do what you will,
Go into business, make money, speculate
In India gold or that synthetic gold from Sardis,
Get rich otherwise than by my consent to bury him.
Teiresias, it is a sorry thing when a wise man
Sells his wisdom, lets out his words for hire!

TEIRESIAS:

Ah Creon! Is there no man left in the world—

CREON:

To do what?—Come, let's have the aphorism!

TEIRESIAS:

No man who knows that wisdom outweighs any
    wealth?

CREON:

As surely as bribes are baser than any baseness.

TEIRESIAS:

You are sick, Creon! You are deathly sick!

CREON:

As you say: it is not my place to challenge a prophet.

TEIRESIAS:

Yet you have said my prophecy is for sale.

CREON:

The generation of prophets has always loved gold.

TEIRESIAS:

The generation of kings has always loved brass.

CREON:

You forget yourself! You are speaking to your King.

TEIRESIAS:

I know it. You are a king because of me.

CREON:

You have a certain skill; but you have sold out.

TEIRESIAS:

King, you will drive me to words that—

CREON:

Say them, say them!
Only remember: I will not pay you for them.

TEIRESIAS:

No, you will find them too costly.

CREON:

No doubt. Speak:
Whatever you say, you will not change my will.

TEIRESIAS:

Then take this, and take it to heart!
The time is not far off when you shall pay back
Corpse for corpse, flesh of your own flesh.

You have thrust the child of this world into living
    night,
You have kept from the gods below the child that is
    theirs:
The one in a grave before her death, the other,
Dead, denied the grave. This is your crime:
And the Furies and the dark gods of Hell
Are swift with terrible punishment for you.

Do you want to buy me now, Creon?

                              Not many days,
And your house will be full of men and women weep-
    ing,
And curses will be hurled at you from far
Cities grieving for sons unburied, left to rot
Before the walls of Thebes.

These are my arrows, Creon: they are all for you.

But come, child: lead me home.   [To BOY:
Let him waste his fine anger upon younger men.
Maybe he will learn at last
To control a wiser tongue in a better head.
                          [Exit TEIRESIAS

CHORAGOS:

The old man has gone, King, but his words
Remain to plague us. I am old, too,
But I cannot remember that he was ever false.

CREON:

That is true. . . . It troubles me.
Oh it is hard to give in! but it is worse
To risk everything for stubborn pride.

CHORAGOS:

Creon: take my advice.

CREON:

What shall I do?

CHORAGOS:

Go quickly: free Antigonê from her vault
And build a tomb for the body of Polyneicês.

CREON:

You would have me do this?

CHORAGOS:

Creon, yes!
And it must be done at once: God moves
Swiftly to cancel the folly of stubborn men.

CREON:

It is hard to deny the heart! But I
Will do it: I will not fight with destiny.

CHORAGOS:

You must go yourself, you cannot leave it to others.

CREON:

I will go.
—Bring axes, servants:
Come with me to the tomb. I buried her, I
Will set her free.
Oh quickly!
My mind misgives—
The laws of the gods are mighty, and a man must
serve them
To the last day of his life!

[*Exit* CREON

◄§ PÆAN

CHORAGOS:

    God of many names   [STROPHE 1

CHORUS:

                O Iacchos
                    son
  of Kadmeian Sémelê
             O born of the Thunder!
  Guardian of the West
            Regent
  of Eleusis' plain
           O Prince of maenad Thebes
  and the Dragon Field by rippling Ismenos:

CHORAGOS:

    God of many names   [ANTISTROPHE 1

CHORUS:

            the flame of torches
  flares on our hills
         the nymphs of Iacchos
  dance at the spring of Castalia:

  from the vine-close mountain
              come ah come in ivy:
  Evohé evohé! sings through the streets of Thebes

CHORAGOS:

    God of many names   [STROPHE 2

CHORUS:

                    Iacchos of Thebes
heavenly Child
                 of Sémelê bride of the Thunderer!
The shadow of plague is upon us:
                                    come
with clement feet
                 oh come from Parnasos
down the long slopes
                    across the lamenting water

CHORAGOS:

                              [ANTISTROPHE 2
Iô Fire! Chorister of the throbbing stars!
O purest among the voices of the night!
Thou son of God, blaze for us!

CHORUS:

Come with choric rapture of circling Maenads
Who cry Iô Iacche!
                 God of many names!

◄§ ÉXODOS

                         [Enter MESSENGER, L.

MESSENGER:

Men of the line of Kadmos, you who live
Near Amphion's citadel:
                    I cannot say
Of any condition of human life "This is fixed,
This is clearly good, or bad". Fate raises up,
And Fate casts down the happy and unhappy alike:

No man can foretell his Fate.
                              Take the case of Creon:
Creon was happy once, as I count happiness:
Victorious in battle, sole governor of the land,
Fortunate father of children nobly born.
And now it has all gone from him! Who can say
That a man is still alive when his life's joy fails?
He is a walking dead man. Grant him rich,
Let him live like a king in his great house:
If his pleasure is gone, I would not give
So much as the shadow of smoke for all he owns.

CHORAGOS:

Your words hint at sorrow: what is your news for us?

MESSENGER:

They are dead. The living are guilty of their death.

CHORAGOS:

Who is guilty? Who is dead? Speak!

MESSENGER:
                              Haimon.
Haimon is dead; and the hand that killed him
Is his own hand.

CHORAGOS:
                    His father's? or his own?

MESSENGER:

His own, driven mad by the murder his father had
     done.

CHORAGOS:

Teiresias, Teiresias, how clearly you saw it all!

MESSENGER:

This is my news: you must draw what conclusions you
     can from it.

CHORAGOS:

But look: Eurydicê, our Queen:
Has she overheard us?

                  [*Enter* EURYDICE *from the Palace,* C.

EURYDICE:

I have heard something, friends:
As I was unlocking the gate of Pallas' shrine,
For I needed her help today, I heard a voice
Telling of some new sorrow. And I fainted
There at the temple with all my maidens about me.
But speak again: whatever it is, I can bear it:
Grief and I are no strangers.

MESSENGER:

                          Dearest Lady,
I will tell you plainly all that I have seen.
I shall not try to comfort you: what is the use,
Since comfort could lie only in what is not true?
The truth is always best.

                      I went with Creon
To the outer plain where Polyneicês was lying,
No friend to pity him, his body shredded by dogs.
We made our prayers in that place to Hecatê
And Pluto, that they would be merciful. And we
    bathed
The corpse with holy water, and we brought
Fresh-broken branches to burn what was left of it,
And upon the urn we heaped up a towering barrow
Of the earth of his own land.

                  When we were done, we ran
To the vault where Antigonê lay on her couch of
    stone.
One of the servants had gone ahead,
And while he was yet far off he heard a voice
Grieving within the chamber, and he came back

And told Creon. And as the King went closer,
The air was full of wailing, the words lost,
And he begged us to make all haste. "Am I a
    prophet?"
He said, weeping, "And must I walk this road,
The saddest of all that I have gone before?
My son's voice calls me on. Oh quickly, quickly!
Look through the crevice there, and tell me
If it is Haimon, or some deception of the gods!"

We obeyed; and in the cavern's farthest corner
We saw her lying:
She had made a noose of her fine linen veil
And hanged herself. Haimon lay beside her,
His arms about her waist, lamenting her,
His love lost under ground, crying out
That his father had stolen her away from him.

When Creon saw him the tears rushed to his eyes
And he called to him: "What have you done, child?
    Speak to me.
What are you thinking that makes your eyes so
    strange?
O my son, my son, I come to you on my knees!"
But Haimon spat in his face. He said not a word,
Staring—
        And suddenly drew his sword
And lunged. Creon shrank back, the blade missed;
    and the boy,
Desperate against himself, drove it half its length
Into his own side, and fell. And as he died
He gathered Antigonê close in his arms again,
Choking, his blood bright red on her white cheek.
And now he lies dead with the dead, and she is his
At last, his bride in the houses of the dead.

             [*Exit* EURYDICE *into the Palace*

CHORAGOS:
    She has left us without a word. What can this mean?

MESSENGER:

It troubles me, too; yet she knows what is best,
Her grief is too great for public lamentation,
And doubtless she has gone to her chamber to weep
For her dead son, leading her maidens in his dirge.

CHORAGOS:

It may be so: but I fear this deep silence

[*Pause*

MESSENGER:

I will see what she is doing. I will go in.

[*Exit* MESSENGER *into the Palace*

[*Enter* CREON *with attendants, bearing*
HAIMON'S *body*

CHORAGOS:

But here is the King himself: oh look at him,
Bearing his own damnation in his arms.

CREON:

Nothing you say can touch me any more.
My own blind heart has brought me
From darkness to final darkness. Here you see
The father murdering, the murdered son—
And all my civic wisdom!

Haimon my son, so young, so young to die,
I was the fool, not you; and you died for me.

CHORAGOS:

That is the truth; but you were late in learning it.

CREON:

This truth is hard to bear. Surely a god
Has crushed me beneath the hugest weight of heaven,

And driven me headlong a barbaric way
To trample out the thing I held most dear.

The pains that men will take to come to pain!
[*Enter* MESSENGER *from the Palace*

MESSENGER:

The burden you carry in your hands is heavy,
But it is not all: you will find more in your house.

CREON:

What burden worse than this shall I find there?

MESSENGER:

The Queen is dead.

CREON:

O port of death, deaf world,
Is there no pity for me? And you, Angel of evil,
I was dead, and your words are death again.
Is it true, boy? Can it be true?
Is my wife dead? Has death bred death?

MESSENGER:

You can see for yourself.
[*The doors are opened, and the body of*
EURYDICE *is disclosed within.*

CREON:

Oh pity!
All true, all true, and more than I can bear!
O my wife, my son!

MESSENGER:

She stood before the altar, and her heart
Welcomed the knife her own hand guided,
And a great cry burst from her lips for Megareus dead,

And for Haimon dead, her sons; and her last breath
Was a curse for their father, the murderer of her sons.
And she fell, and the dark flowed in through her clos-
  ing eyes

CREON:

O God, I am sick with fear.
Are there no swords here? Has no one a blow for me?

MESSENGER:

Her curse is upon you for the deaths of both.

CREON:

It is right that it should be. I alone am guilty.
I know it, and I say it. Lead me in,
Quickly, friends.
I have neither life nor substance. Lead me in.

CHORAGOS:

You are right, if there can be right in so much wrong.
The briefest way is best in a world of sorrow.

CREON:

Let it come,
Let death come quickly, and be kind to me.
I would not ever see the sun again.

CHORAGOS:

All that will come when it will; but we, meanwhile,
Have much to do. Leave the future to itself.

CREON:

All my heart was in that prayer!

CHORAGOS:

Then do not pray any more: the sky is deaf.

CREON:

Lead me away. I have been rash and foolish.
I have killed my son and my wife.
I look for comfort; my comfort lies here dead.
Whatever my hands have touched has come to noth-
 ing.
Fate has brought all my pride to a thought of dust.
> [As CREON *is being led into the house, the*
> CHORAGOS *advances and speaks directly to*
> *the audience*

CHORAGOS:

There is no happiness where there is no wisdom;
No wisdom but in submission to the gods.
Big words are always punished,
And proud men in old age learn to be wise.

◀§ COMMENTARY

> *Et quod propriè dicitur in idiomate Picardorum hor-*
> *rescit apud Burgundos, immò apud Gallicos vici-*
> *niores; quanto igitur magis accidet hoc apud linguas*
> *diversas! Quapropter quod bene factum est in unâ*
> *linguâ non est possibile ut transferatur in aliam*
> *secundum ejus proprietatem quam habuerit in priori.*
> ROGER BACON

I. In the Commentary appended to our version of Euripides' *Alcestis* we wrote: "Our object was to make the
Alcestis clear and credible in English. Since it is a poem,
it had to be made clear as a poem; and since it is a
play, it had to be made credible as a play. We set for
ourselves no fixed rules of translation or of dramatic
verse: often we found the best English equivalent in a
literalness which extended to the texture and rhythm of
the Greek phrasing; at other times we were forced to a
more or less free paraphrase in order to achieve effects
which the Greek conveyed in ways impossible to English. Consequently, this version of the *Alcestis* is not a
'translation' in the classroom sense of the word. The
careful reader, comparing our text with the original, will
discover alterations, suppressions, expansions—a word,
perhaps, drawn out into a phrase, or a phrase condensed
to a word: a way of saying things that is admittedly not
Euripidean, if by Euripidean one means a translation
ad verbum expressa of Euripides' poem. In defense we
can say only that our purpose was to reach—and, if possible, to render precisely—the emotional and sensible
meaning in every speech in the play; we could not fol-

low the Greek word for word, where to do so would have been weak and therefore false." We have been guided by the same principles in making this version of the *Antigonê*.

II. We have made cuts only when it seemed absolutely necessary. The most notable excision is that of a passage of sixteen lines beginning with 904 (Antigonê's long speech near the end of Scene IV), which has been bracketed as spurious, either in whole or in part, by the best critics. Aristotle quotes two verses from it, which proves, as Professor Jebb points out, that if it is an interpolation it must have been made soon after Sophocles' death, possibly by his son Iophon. However that may be, it is dismal stuff. Antigonê is made to interrupt her lamentation by a series of limping verses whose sense is as discordant as their sound. We quote the Oxford Translation, the style of which is for once wholly adequate to the occasion:

And yet, in the opinion of those who have just sentiments, I honoured you [Polyneicês] aright. For neither, though I had been the mother of children, nor though my husband dying, had mouldered away, would I have undertaken this toil against the will of the citizens. On account of what law do I say this? There would have been another husband for me if the first died, and if I lost my child there would have been another from another man! but my father and my mother being laid in the grave, it is impossible a brother should ever be born to me. On the principle of such a law, having preferred you, my brother, to all other considerations, I seemed to Creon to commit a sin, and to dare what was dreadful. And now, seizing me by force, he thus leads me away, having never enjoyed the nuptial bed, nor heard the nuptial lay, nor having gained the lot of marriage, nor of rearing my children; but thus I, an unhappy woman, deserted by my friends, go, while alive, to the cavern of the dead.

There are other excisions of less importance. Perhaps the discussion of one of them will serve to explain them all. Near the end of the *Éxodos*, Creon is told of his wife's suicide. The Messenger has five very graphic lines describing Eurydicê's suicide, to which Creon responds with an outburst of dread and grief; yet two lines later, as if he had not heard the first time, he is asking the Messenger how Eurydicê died. The Messenger replies that she stabbed herself to the heart. There is no evidence that the question and reply are interpolations: on the contrary, they serve the definite purpose of filling out the iambic interlude between two lyric strophes; but in a modern version which does not attempt to reproduce the strophic structure of this *Kommós* they merely clog the dialogue. Therefore we have skipped them; and the occasional suppression of short passages throughout the play is based upon similar considerations.

III. In a like manner, we have not hesitated to use free paraphrase when a literal rendering of the Greek would result in obscurity. Again, the discussion of a specific instance may illuminate the whole question.

After Antigonê has been led away to death, the Chorus, taking a hint from her having compared her own fate to that of Niobê, proceeds to elaborate the stories of mythological persons who have suffered similar punishment. The Fourth Ode cites Danaê, Lycurgos, the son of Dryas, and Cleopatra, the daughter of Boreas and wife of the Thracian king Phineus. Only Danaê is mentioned by name; the others are allusively identified. The difficulty arises from the allusive method. Sophocles' audience would be certain to recognize the allusions, but that is not true of ours. To what extent can we depend upon the audience's recognition in a day when, to quote Mr. I. A. Richards, "we can no longer refer with any confidence to any episode in the Bible, or to any nursery tale or any piece of mythology"? We can assume that the story of Danaê is still current; but Lycurgos is forgotten now, and the sordid Phineus-Cleopatra-Eidothea affair no longer stirs so much as an echo. Nevertheless, Sophocles devotes two of his four strophes to this Cleopatra, and he does it in so oblique a manner that 'translation' is out of the question. We have therefore rendered these strophes with such slight additions to the Greek sense as might convey an equivalent suggestion of fable to a modern audience.

IV. The Chorus is composed, says the Scholiast, of "certain old men of Thebes": leading citizens ("O men many-charioted, in love with Fortune") to whom Creon addresses his fatal decree, and from whom he later takes advice. Sophocles' Chorus numbered fifteen, including the Choragos, or Leader; its function was to chant the Odes and, in the person of the Choragos, to participate in the action. In a version designed for the modern stage certain changes are inevitable. It cannot be urged too strongly that the words of the Odes must be intelligible to the audience; and they are almost certain not to be intelligible if they are chanted in unison by so large a group, with or without musical accompaniment. It is suggested, then, that in producing this play no attempt be made to follow the ancient choric method. There should be no dancing. The *Párodos*, for example, should be a solemn but almost unnoticeable evolution of moving or still patterns accompanied by a drum-beat whose rhythm may be derived from the cadence of the Ode itself. The lines given to the Chorus in the Odes should probably be spoken by single voices. The only accompaniment should be percussion: we follow Allan Sly's score of the *Alcestis* in suggesting a large side drum from which the snares have been removed, to be struck with two felt-headed tympani sticks, one hard, one soft.

V. A careful production might make successful use of masks. They should be of the Benda type used in the production of O'Neill's *The Great God Brown*: lifelike, closely fitting the contours of the face, and valuable only as they give the effect of immobility to character. On no account should there be any attempt to reproduce the Greek mask, which was larger than life size and served a function non-existent on the modern stage—the amplification of voice and mood for projection to the distant seats of the outdoor theater.

If masks are used at all, they might well be allotted only to those characters who are somewhat depersonalized by official position or discipline: Creon, Teiresias, the Chorus and Choragos, possibly the Messenger. By this rule, Antigonê has no mask; neither has Ismenê, Haimon, nor Eurydicê. If Creon is masked, we see no objection, in art or feeling, to the symbolic removal of his mask before he returns with the dead body of his son

We cannot let our *Antigonê* go without expressing our gratitude to those friends who have been so helpful to us in many ways: to Eleanor Green and Horace Gregory and Arthur Mizener for their acute criticism; to Margaret Goodwin, whose theater-sense has been the relentless corrective of our poetry; and to Lydia Hewitt for the patience with which she made revision upon revision in the task of preparing the final manuscript.

DF
RF

All Souls Day : 1938

❧ INDEX OF NAMES

The transliteration of Greek names is an uncertain and—ultimately, perhaps—subjective matter. Certain of the entries below have more than one form, the first being that used in this translation.

ARTEMIS: goddess of the hunt, sister of Apollo

ATALANTA: an Arcadian princess, mother of PARTHENO-
PAEUS, *q.v.*

ATHENA, ATHENE: daughter of Zeus; tutelary goddess of
Athens

BACCHOS: a name for DIONYSOS, *q.v.*

CAPANEUS: one of the seven Captains supporting Polyneicês against Eteoclês

CASTALIA: a spring sacred to the Muses, on Mount Parnassos

COLONUS, KOLONOS: a deme of Attica, near Athens

CREON, KREON: brother of IOCASTE, *q.v.*; father of HAIMON
and MEGAREUS, *qq.v.*; King of Thebes after the death
of Polyneicês and Eteoclês

DANAE: a princess of Argos, confined by her father in a
brazen chamber underground (or, some say, in a
brazen tower), where she was seduced by Zeus in the
form of a golden rain, and bore him Perseus

DAULIA, DAULIS: a city of Phokis

DELPHI, DELPHOI: a city of Phokis; seat of a celebrated
Oracle of Apollo

DEMETER: a sister of Zeus; goddess of agriculture

DIONYSOS: son of Zeus and SEMELE, *q.v.*; god of wine

DIRCE, DIRKE: a spring near Thebes

DRYAS: a king of Thrace; father of Lykûrgos, who was
driven mad by Dionysos

ELEUSIS: a city in Attica, sacred to Demêter and Persephonê; hence, adj., ELEUSINIAN

ELIS: a city in the Peloponnesos, noted for its horses and
for a shrine of Zeus

ETEOCLES, ETEOKLES: a son of Oedipus and Iocastê;
brother of POLYNEICES, *q.v.*

ETEOCLUS, ETEOKLOS: one of the seven Captains supporting Polyneicês in the Theban expedition; killed at
Thebes by MEGAREUS, *q.v.*

EUMENIDES: 'The Gracious Ones': euphemistically for
the FURIES, *q.v.*

MAENAD: a priestess of DIONYSOS, *q.v.*

MEGAREUS: a son of CREON, *q.v.*; died during the assault of the Seven against Thebes

MENOIKEUS: father of CREON and IOCASTE, *qq.v.*

MEROPE: wife of King Polybos of Corinth; foster-mother of Oedipus

MUSES: nine daughters of Zeus and the nymph Mnemosynê; goddesses presiding over the arts and sciences

NAUSIKAA: a daughter of King Alkinoös of Scheria, who befriended Odysseus

NIOBE: wife of AMPHION, *q.v.*; mother of fourteen children killed, because of her pride, by Apollo and Artemis; transformed into a rock on Mt. Sipylos

OEDIPUS: son of LAIOS and IOCASTE, *qq.v.*

OINEUS: an Aetolian king, father of TYDEUS, *q.v.*

OLYMPOS, OLYMPUS: a Thessalian mountain; the seat of the gods

PALLAS: an epithet of ATHENA, *q.v.*

PAN: an Arcadian rural god

PARNASSOS, PARNASOS, PARNASSUS: a mountain sacred to Apollo; at its foot are Delphi and the Castalian Spring

PARTHENOPAEUS, PARTHENOPAIOS: one of the seven Captains supporting Polyneicês in the Theban campaign

PELOPS: a son of Tantalos; father of ATREUS, *q.v.*

PERSEPHONE: daughter of DEMETER, *q.v.*; Queen of Hades

PHASIS: a river in Colchis emptying into the Black Sea

PHOIBOS, PHOEBUS: an epithet of APOLLO, *q.v.*

PHOKIS: a kingdom on the Gulf of Corinth

PIRITHOUS, PEIRITHOOS, PIRITHOOS: a chieftain of the Lapithai; old friend of THESEUS, *q.v.*

PLUTO: brother of Zeus and Poseidon; King of Hades

POLYBOS: King of Corinth; foster-father of Oedipus

POLYDOROS: a son of KADMOS, *q.v.*; great-grandfather of Oedipus

POLYNEICES, POLYNEIKES: a son of Oedipus and Iocastê; killed by his brother Eteoclês, whom he killed at the same time, during the assault upon Thebes

PYTHIAN: an epithet of Apollo as Oracle at Delphi
[Πυθώ]

SARDIS: a city in Lydia

SEMELE: a daughter of KADMOS, q.v.; mother, by Zeus, of
the god Dionysos

SPHINX: a riddling she-monster who killed herself when
Oedipus solved her riddle

TALAUS, TALAOS: cited in the text, erroneously, as father
of HIPPOMEDON, q.v.

TANTALOS, TANTALUS: a king of Phrygia; father of PELOPS
and NIOBE, qq.v.

TEIRESIAS, TIRESIAS: a blind prophet of Thebes; counsellor
of Oedipus and Creon

THESEUS: King of Athens; son of AEGEUS, q.v.

TYDEUS: one of the seven Captains supporting Polyneices
in the Theban campaign, and the only one to survive

ZEUS: father of gods and men

πόνος πόνῳ πόνον φέρει.
πᾷ πᾷ
πᾷ γὰρ οὐκ ἔβαν ἐγώ;